REDEEMING CULTURE

~THE OTHER SIDE OF THE COIN~

Velma D. White

PRESS

Copyright © 2008 by Velma D. White

Redeeming Culture – The Other Side of The Coin
by Velma D. White

Printed in the United States of America

ISBN 978-1-60477-706-2

Unless otherwise indicated, Bible quotations are taken from The King James/Amplified Bible Parallel Edition Grand Rapids, Michigan 49530, U.S.A., Copyright © 1995 by Zondervan Corporation, and The Amplified Bible, Copyright © 1954, 1958, 1962, 1964, 1965, 1987 by The Lockman Foundation, (www.Lockman.org), and The Holy Bible, New Life Version, Copyright © 1969, 1976, 1978, 1983, 1986, by Christian Literature, International, P.O. Box 777, Canby, OR 97013. Used by permission.

Editors:
Loathar Menche
Glenna Cummings
Lori Byers
Jane Martin

www.xulonpress.com

Thanks:

I would like to express my thanks first of all to Jesus my, Lord and Savior, for writing my name in the Lamb's Book of Life and for all He has done for me.

I would also like to thank Lothar, Glenna, Lori and Jane for all their time and effort in working with me to make this book happen! Thanks for believing in me!

Dedication:

This book is dedicated to the glory of God the Father, God the Son and God the Holy Ghost!

In loving memory of:

Larry Stewart, 1935-2007

PROLOGUE

It was a cloudy, grey afternoon over the Chateau
Lake Louise. The cold wind blew off the mountains and beat against the high walls outside of the
hotel. Spring had finally come. It was nice to get
outside and to catch a breath of the fresh mountain air. I had been living in Calgary and had just
completed my first year of Bible College. I was
glad that it was over; it had not been an easy year
for me. I had moved from the reservation to a city
where I hardly knew a soul. I encountered many spiritual battles, not to mention the cultural change and
adjustments I had to make, but I refused to give up. I
was determined that I was going to serve God. Here
I was, now attending a Woman's Conference at this
beautiful hotel where service is a Five Star rating!
I had never thought I would be in such an "upper
class" place where only the wealthy could afford to
come. I felt like a princess. Some time earlier, one of
my teachers from Bible College prayed for me and

as he prayed, he began to speak as the Spirit of God gave him utterance. I clearly remember him speaking as though God were speaking through him, "*You are mine! You are my princess! I am your Chief!...*". Those words rang so loudly in my ears as my eyes filled with tears. Princess? Me? *His* princess? Why me? I had such low self esteem and did not feel worth a whole lot. By the summer of that year it would have been two years since I had rededicated my life to God. I knew then it would not be an easy road. I was only 18, and in the community where I grew up, not many young people my age would continue to follow Jesus. Life was not easy on the reserve. Being a Christian seemed more difficult because it was a lonely road. I was not faithful to the Lord in my High School years. When I had finally made the decision to follow Him, I knew that I was turning my back on the world and the friends I loved. I knew they would not follow. The "party" life had taken hold of them, but I was determined to break free from the cycle of alcoholism and "back sliding". This time my decision for God was a "no turning back" decision. Realizing how often I had failed God, I desperately asked for His help, for I knew that without His help, I could not live a life that was pleasing to Him.

"*Princess?*" I thought as I stood outside of the hotel, "*I wonder what God's plan for my life will be?*" I made my way back inside to get out of the cold wind. I went over to the banqueting hall where our scheduled supper was. There my other friends, whom I had come to know and love since moving to Calgary, were already seated at one of the round tables. One of the ladies whom I had met around the same time I had rededicated my life to Lord, was also there. As we conversed about the goodness of God, she kept watching me. She made me a little nervous, but I felt the Lord was showing her something, though I dared not ask what. Finally she called me from across the table. She asked, "*Have you ever worshipped the eagle?*" Stunned, I replied, "*Well, yeah, sort of.*" I further explained that the eagle was the god over the reserve I came from and there the eagle was very much worshipped. In fact on the outside wall of one of the main buildings is written in big bold letters, "*Kihew-Manitou*" meaning, "*the eagle is god*". There was a time in my early teens when my heart was hard against God and Christianity. I had dabbled with satanic worship and looked to the wind and eagle as gods. At age 14, I had an encounter with the Living God and had given my heart back to Him. I threw away my occult objects of false worship and secular heavy metal music, yet still I had an attraction to eagles. I often had posters of eagles, especially ones associated with Harley-Davidson clothing. Although I had given my heart back to Jesus, rebellion still had a strong grip in my soul. When at age 18, I had rededicated my life back to the Lord; I had not changed my rebellious attitude. Most of it was to resist "*religiosity*". I hated religion and legalism. I had been very hurt by it in the Christian school I attended from grade four to seven. My favorite type of jewelry had become eagle feathers and eagle figures.

When that lady asked me the question *"Have you ever worshipped the eagle?"* all I could say was *"Yes, sort of."* She then explained why she asked, *"I saw an eagle's claw on top of your head and I saw that your eyes are the same as eagle's eyes. Perhaps you need to renounce the eagle spirit. If you have any jewelry that represents the eagle, you should throw it away."* Deep in my spirit, I knew she was right. Perhaps this was the answer to why I struggled so much in Bible College. I did not do so well that year, and it showed in my grades. I had many battles with evil spirits in my sleep and often barely made it to class because of tiredness. It had not occurred to me that to disassociate with things that represented a false god that I had once worshipped would bring me greater freedom in my Christian walk. I asked the lady to pray for me. She came to the empty chair beside me and in prayer broke the "generational curse" of the eagle spirit off me. She then blew on my eyes and commanded the spirit to go. After we finished our meal I ran to my hotel room.

On the way there, a friend of mine from Bible College met me in the elevator. Her eyes grew big as she looked at me. I smiled nervously and said, *"What?"* She said, *"Your eyes look different!"* I knew then that the lady who had prayed for me was on track and that God was telling me what I should do. I explained to my friend what had occurred at the dinner table and what I was going to do next, and I asked her to accompany me. When I got in my hotel room, I went through my bag, found all my eagle feather jewelry, gathered them in my hand and then my friend and I went to the lookout right above the lake.

"*Make it fast, it's freezing!*" she said, as she shivered and folded her arms tight in front of her to keep her warm. The wind was still blowing off the mountains and the grey clouds continued to cover the sky above us. The sun had not shone the whole day. I took my jewelry and threw it on the ground and began to smash each piece with the heel of my leather boot. I then picked up each piece, tossed it all into the frozen Lake Louise, and I then began to shout, "*I renounce you eagle spirit! You are not my god! Jesus is my Lord and Savior and I worship Him alone in spirit and in truth!*" Just at that moment, a hole appeared in the clouds and a ray of the sun shone through on us giving us warmth from the cold wind. I knew that the Lord Jesus had heard my declaration and had confirmed to me that He was honoring what I was doing. "*Wow! Look! The sun is shining upon us!*" said my friend who was with me. I stood there with her, enjoying the warmth it gave us both. We both knew that the S O N was shining on us. Within the next moment the clouds covered the hole; rejoicing in the Lord, we made our way back to the hotel.

"*Yes, it is true!*" I thought, "*I do belong to the Lord!*" I began to realize that perhaps God had consecrated my life. As His Word says, before He formed the world He knew us. I knew then in my heart that God really did have a plan and a purpose for me.

PART ONE

INTRODUCTION
~ AN IDENTITY CRISIS~

At age 14 the Lord God revealed Himself to me by His sweet voice at a time when I was not seeking Him. I was angry at God and hated Christianity. I had turned my back on God and pursued devil worship out of spite against God and anything to do with Him. Rebellion and hatred took hold of my heart. Since this was my mind set at the time, why then would God reveal His love and mercy to me and speak to me? The scriptures say that "He was found among a people that sought Him not"[1]. That included me! I sought Him not, yet His love melted the hardness in my heart. After an incredible encounter with God, I was radically changed! I was immediately filled with the Spirit of God. He was all I thought about at that time. I wrote many poems about His love. I knew that I was forgiven. What a joy that filled my heart! I vowed I would not harden my heart again nor would I ever turn to another god.

The remainder of my teen years brought many hardships and temptations, and I regret to say that I was not faithful to the Lord. I experimented with drugs and alcohol and found them to be a comfort and an easy way to forget the hardships I faced. Basically, I felt sorry for myself and would not turn to God for strength. In the middle of these back-sliding years, I would often go to places where my faith in God would be strengthened and I would give it "a good try" to stop smoking, drinking, and doing drugs. I'd last a while and then "fall away" again. Without realizing it, I became part of a cycle that is a curse to many of our Native people. I was trapped and wanted to break free!

At age 18, I left the reserve, my family and friends and found myself at the back of my friend's apartment building smoking a cigarette outside. I was about to head out to a tent meeting that she invited me to. I decided to have two cigarettes in case the service was too long before my next craving could be satisfied. It makes me laugh just thinking about it now. As I sat there smoking, I was contemplating my life and wondering if I could "make a break" with it or not; would it be worth trying? Then I heard that same sweet voice that I had encountered when I was 14, only this time it was stern, *"Choose this day whom you will serve. Do not put me out like a cigarette!"* I was afraid to put out the cigarette I was smoking. I replied, *"Lord, I need your help! I can't do it! I try and I always fail. Please show me how to be a good Christian.*" I then rose up from the ground and walked to the garbage can and threw my cigarettes and lighter into it. That night I went forward when they gave the altar call and I rededicated my life to the Lord. I felt God's power in a real way. I wept as I felt Him wash over me with His Spirit. My body shook uncontrollably as I felt His touch. I knew that this time things really were going to be different. Something had changed inwardly and my relationship with the Lord was restored. That took place near the end of the month of June in 1993 in the city of Red Deer on 67St. N. From that point on, my walk with God has intensified. I love Him because He first loved me, and my love for Him has grown immensely.

A week later a certain lady was ministering to me in prayer and felt the need to repent on behalf of the white people for the injustices done to my people. This seemed unnecessary to me for I knew she was not a part of what had happened in the history of our people. I did not understand, but, to be polite, I accepted her apology and told her I forgave her. The whole time I was feeling awkward about her apology. I did recall in that moment the historical facts, taught to us in school and orally at home, of the injustices done to our people. I remember a field trip during high school, my Cree teacher took our class on. It was a tour through one of the residential schools she had attended as a child. She took us through the building one floor at a time into every room as she recalled her memories there as a student. As we walked through the school with her, the reality of what our people went through began to sink in. I carried a grudge towards white people and the government for the things that had gone on and felt that our people had not received justice. However, this lady, who repented in proxy of the white people, was a Christian, and I did not hold this grudge against her, so her apology did not make sense to me.

As time went on, I found myself, at age 20, in the middle of a reconciliation service in a small hamlet in Alberta. One of my spiritual leaders stood in front of the group of Native people whom he had called to stand in front of the congregation. He recited the injustices done to our people and with tears began repenting and asking for forgiveness on behalf of the white people. As this was going on, I found myself bent over on the floor weeping and wailing with the pain that I felt for my people. It was too much to bear. I felt God take out the bitterness in my heart towards the white people. I hadn't even realized how deeply prejudice and racism was entrenched in my heart until that moment. The microphone was passed over to me and all I could do was say that, "*On behalf of the Cree people I forgive you.*" I did not know the right protocol or terminology to use as I spoke on behalf of the Cree people. Then another Cree fellow took the microphone and replied from his heart and released forgiveness on behalf of the Native people in general.

That night I thought a lot about that service. I began to have some understanding why that lady, two years earlier, had made a similar apology to me in proxy for the white people. A few weeks earlier I had become fully aware that God was calling me to minister to my own people and He began to shape in me a heart for it. At the time, I did not want to go back to the reservation (or any other reservations) because of my bitter past growing up there. I had other plans. I was going into ministry with inner city youth and some day would be a singer. What I foresaw for my life in the ministry was not in God's plan. He had a better one which is still unfolding!

A few weeks prior to that reconciliation service, I had received a vision from the Lord. In this vision, I saw a giant teepee with holy fire from heaven being poured into it like water coming out of a faucet. There were two angels standing on either side of this teepee. They were much taller than the teepee itself and I could hear the angels singing songs of worship to God, such as I have never heard on earth before or since. I then saw dark figures of human beings walking into the tent with heavy loads on their backs. As they entered the teepee, these heavy loads fell off, and in the next instant, they would exit all pure, clean, and free with God's holy fire all over them. They were going out to spread this holy fire from heaven that was being poured into the teepee. After receiving this vision, I realized that God was speaking to me about what He is about to do among the Native people of this land. He showed me a teepee because it represented this particular people group, the Native people. As the Bible says, "In the last days I will pour out of my Spirit upon all flesh..."[2] It was then clear to me that He is about to pour out His Spirit upon my people. This excited me! It gave me great hope as I began to involve myself in several ministries, from Bible camps to church fellowships and evangelical outreach, ministering to Native people.

At age 22 I became an intern for a Native fellowship for a short time. During those days I found myself, again, in the middle of another reconciliation service. This time it was the spiritual leaders and fathers repenting to "Generation X" (which consisted of young people under the age of 25), for hurting them spiritually. I was standing there on the platform in the middle of the "Generation X" age group (of which I was included at the time). Upon hearing the leaders and fathers' repentance, again, I found myself on the floor weeping and wailing. This repentance touched the core of a painful memory of my past that had to do with the Christian school I attended as a child. That day God began a work of healing that still goes on today.

After these significant events occurred in my life, I began to understand in a greater measure why the Lord used that lady to introduce to me the concept of reconciliation. God used it to begin a healing process that included forgiving those that had hurt me. I have learned that healing does not come without releasing forgiveness to those that have offended us in all areas of our lives, whether spiritually or physically. As I had also suffered physical and sexual abuse as a child growing up, abuse seemed to be a normal part of life to me. Over time, God has brought me through a great deal of healing regarding various incidents that occurred in my life. I understand His grace, love and mercy in such a way that I can't help but live my life for Him. He is near to those who have a broken heart! My heart is not broken now the way it was when I rededicated my life to Him at age 18. Then I did not walk with my head up, I hardly smiled; life was so serious to me. I was determined to be a strong person and to let no one hurt me. That too changed! The Lord is now the Lifter of my head, the Lover of my soul, the Healer of my heart, my Strength, my Redeemer, my Refuge, my Joy and the One in whom I put my trust! None can compare to Him. I yearn for a closer walk with Him every day! Once, when I was 15, I went to church with my mother on the reserve. As we waited for the service to begin, I noticed a song book that belonged to the church. At that time I was not familiar with the songs in that church. As I flipped through the pages of the song book, I came across the words of, "Just A Closer Walk With Thee". Those words were so beautiful to me; they seemed to say what I was feeling at the time, for I was not as close to God as I wanted to be and had been a few months earlier. I wanted to know how the song sounded. Just then the pastor asked if any one had a special song they wanted him to lead us in, so I requested that one. It has since become my favorite song as it continues to express the cry of my heart.

I began a search for truth in God's Word about what it means to be a Christian, or rather a native Christian, in today's world. I wanted to walk close to God continually. I began to evaluate my walk and search out God's Word. At first, I had shunned all practices of the traditions of my people, initially knowing that these do not agree with God's Word.

How I knew this was definitely a witness of the Spirit teaching and leading me in my walk with God. After all, as I thought about it, how could using that which I had used to worship and cause other spirits to manifest bring glory to the living God whom I was now serving and loving with all my heart? I only wanted to honor and bring attention and praise to Him alone. Later, however, after being introduced to the idea of redeeming native cultural traditions such as drum and dance for Christian worship, I began to take up "the cause". I danced in traditional regalia to the sound of the sacred drum hoping to honor the Creator- Jesus with this form of worship. For the sake of the healing of my people, I came to believe that the redemption of native culture through Christianity cannot be ignored. I often spoke out about it and managed to convince the majority of those within my sphere of influence that this was so. I used random scriptures in God's Word as the basis for my arguments. During my search for truth, two friends made statements that impacted me greatly. The first stated, *"The cross will always confront our culture, no matter what culture we come from"*. The other stated, *"Christ came to redeem the person, not the culture"*. These two statements hit me both in my spirit and in my way of thinking and challenged my mindset to the core. With a sincere heart I began to seek the Lord for guidance and began to ask Him to reveal His word to me in such a way that I would really know His truth. I then made a mental decision to lay aside my own ideas and other people's opinions regarding the matter of redeeming native culture and traditions for Christian worship. As I began a thorough search through God's Word (which still goes on today), my eyes began to open to the reality of what Christ had accomplished on the cross for mankind. As I sought God and His Word, I began to see "the other side of the coin" regarding the redemption of culture and syncretism. (I will share this more in detail in the section entitled, *"Cultural Identity in Christ – Why are we having an identity crisis?"* and throughout the remains of this book.) However, as I earnestly sought the Lord, I began to realize that I did not need to go back to the traditions of my people to find out who I am as a Christian Native or to receive healing. Instead, I need to pursue Christ and to follow all that He is, to walk in His ways and to live for Him. I came to this conclusion based on God's Holy Word and invite you to share in my journey.

I am now living in the NWT as a missionary with two other ladies. Both are pastors and head the ministry that I am with. I have been traveling and ministering with them, since the summer of 2000. As I type this, my black leather Bible is beside me and the significance of its color has real meaning and purpose for me as it was prophesied by our elders long ago that men of another race would come with a black book to show our people the way of life.[3]

The Lord has taken me on an incredible journey since the time of that second reconciliation service. So far I have gone to many Native villages across Northwestern Canada (western provinces and territories) including down the West Coast, and also into Alaska. I have seen the Spirit of God move among my people in incredible ways. Yet, in other places, I have seen little response to the Gospel and I know why it is so. Many of my Native people carry what I lived under: pain, grief, anger, bitterness, addiction, abuse, rage, racism, prejudice, hatred, false religion, fear, superstitions, betrayal, and the list goes on. Many are currently in the process (and have been for many years now) of revitalizing their cultural traditions in light of spirituality and identity. When Native people speak of tradition and culture they do not mean just arts and crafts and making bannock; they are also talking of their religion, and they identify this as their spirituality. Their spirituality permeates every area of their lives. For example, when the clothing is used for dances and ceremonies, these items go through spiritual ceremonies before they are used and/or sold to others for use. As many of the Native people had to adapt to the environment around them and most of this generation does not know their own native language, the schools on the reservations and other Native communities are making great efforts to re-educate today's generation in their language and culture. This not only includes hunting, fishing, trapping, learning to make moccasins and tan hides, but it also has a great deal to do with spirituality (religious practices of Native religion). When referring to "culture", our people are mainly thinking of the traditional religion of the sacred drum with all its components, which touches every aspect of their life and being.

During the year that I received the vision of the teepee from the Lord, I came across a book[4] that gives

the history of my people when true men of God came
to my people so long ago. It helped me to understand
a lot of things. I learned that there were missionaries
who came in the early days who truly did care for
the Native people. Many lived through extreme hardships; some also have laid down their lives to bring
the Word of God to my people and to show them the
true love of God and His way. I came to realize that
the Anglican, United and Roman Catholic Church
were not the only churches that sent missionaries to
my people. Along with those who truly cared, there
were, however, those from these and other denominations that were sadly known for sexual abuse and
many other injustices which were done to my people.
These injustices caused us to loose our innocence,
dignity, long hair, identity, language and culture.
Today they have apologized for what occurred in
the past and the government is endeavoring to make
restitution. Many caring white people have felt guilt
and sorrow for what happened years ago.

We are now seeing the pendulum swing far to the
other side; this is creating other problems. Some of
the White churches are inviting Native traditions to
be practiced in their services, often due to the feeling
of guilt and/or regret for the crimes done to my people
at the hands of many of their clergy in the past. They
want to somehow make amends. However, in trying
to make amends in this way, often, they open their
doors to the worship and influence of other gods in
their sanctuaries, and now willingly open the way for
syncretism (the practice of two religions operating in
the unseen). This *cultural* emphasis (rather than the

emphasis being on becoming more like Jesus), often causes confusion and, at times, it causes contention. It has been a stumbling block to many of those seeking new life in Christ. Along with difficulties stemming from syncretism there are also, at the same time, some evangelists going to reserves, who misrepresent the Gospel of Christ in the areas of immorality. Others exploit the people as they manipulate and take up huge offerings as though it were some auction. Incredibly, some of these self-proclaimed evangelists are Native! These things combined with the increasing emphasis on initializing native culture (which to Native people includes their spirituality), has truly left many of my people wondering what Christianity is all about.

However, regardless of how the pendulum is swinging, I have found that it is important to remember that God *has* sent (and is still sending) true men and women of God as missionaries to our people. These God sent missionaries (native or white) are proclaiming the *true* Gospel of Christ and Christianity as seen in the life, and not just talked about from the pulpit. Of course, this is seldom recorded in secular history. Rather, it is shared by oral tradition. With the aid of God's Word, research and the Lord's guidance in my spiritual journey, I have come to understand more of the spiritual history of our people. This understanding of our history has been key to helping me understand not only more about the culture of my people, but also relevant issues, such as the redemption of culture and syncretism. I invite you to share this journey with me.

PART TWO

YESTURDAY AND TODAY

Norman Taylor, in his book, "My book, My People, Our Kingdom", shares the following story which was passed down orally among his people.[5] (From this point I will be going back and forth between oral tradition and stories related through Norman Taylor.)

In His book, Norman Taylor tells of how a very long time ago, there were several native tribes (including the Cree) that had begun to seek the Creator, or the Great Spirit for the way of life. The Lord God's name was not known to our ancestors. Every year feasts were held and during these feasts, spiritual times were set aside as the people began searching for the way of life by means of ceremonies including medicine men and their initiates. Although this did not help their search, our ancestors continued to seek because they felt spiritually empty and longed for the meaning of life. Then one day, during a cere-mony, the Spirit of God appeared to these ancestors and revealed that He would send a man from another race with a Black Book in which would be the words of life. They were to receive him and he would show them the Words of the Creator. This prophecy was held throughout the generations as God prepared their hearts for the right people to come to them[6].

Oral tradition tells us that when the white settlers came to this land, our native ancestors assisted these early settlers by teaching them survival skills, thus sparing them from starvation. Overtime, as more settlers came and saw the vast resources of the lands in which the native people dwelt, they began to send word back to their homelands, inviting others to join them in exploring and settling in this great continent with all its wealth. However, one thing was not considered: there were already people of many languages living on this continent from days of old. The newcomers called our ancestors Natives, or Indians and often savages.

Amongst these white settlers were people of the Christian faith who were called by God to spread His Gospel to the tribal peoples of the land. Most were not part of any large denomination, but simply had a heart for God and had a real burden to share the Way of Life with our people in order that they, too, could have the same joy of knowing Jesus, the Son of God. We know that Satan, the enemy of God and His people, competes for the souls of all mankind. However, God, in His sovereignty, was working through these true believers, in spite of the ambitious greed that was prevalent among many of the white settlers of that day. Over time the greed began to grow. Other people, who said they cared about the Native people and the gospel, also began to come. However, caring about the Native people and the gospel often was not the case. Although some claimed to follow these believers in endeavoring to share the Gospel of Christ with the Native people, others had ulterior motives[7]. As one Native elder, thinking about those days, said to me, "The white settlers came with a Bible in one hand and when they saw the timber, copper and fish, they put the Bible down and went after the resources. At least they left us with God's Word!" That is a perfect way of describing what happened. Not only was religion affected by the reports of prosperity in the new land, so were the politics of the day.

As a result, the French and the English began to make war for sovereignty over the land they occupied. Many Native tribes fought to keep their territory, but were unsuccessful and were forced out of the way by the power of the guns wielded by these white settlers.

Oral tradition related that after the English won the war, and the French surrendered, the English began to go after the Native tribes in order to conquer more land and to make it theirs. This of course caused great animosity between the Native tribes and the white settlers. Our ancestors fought hard to keep their territory, and in the end came to surrender for the sake of the survival of their people. Consequently, they signed peace treaties with the Government of that day. The treaties were meant to last "as long as the grass grows and the rivers run"[8]. War over land was never in God's plan; it was the work of the evil one who always tries to thwart God's purposes and to resist God's people. This was spiritual warfare at the heart of it all. Yet still, God turns all things around for good. He is Lord of the battle and brings Satan's plans to naught.

As things began to settle in the land, men of God again began to come to our ancestors and to share the Way of Life with them. In spite of the warfare against the white settlers, our ancestors still held fast to the prophecy of old that someone from another race would come with the Black Book and share the Way of Life with them. Some of our ancestors wondered, perhaps, if there was such a man among the white settlers that had already come to their land.

I learned through oral tradition, the Hudson Bay Company had many fur-trading posts set up all over the Canada of that day. There, our ancestors would trade their furs with the white settlers for guns and necessities, etc. The Cree were like middlemen between other tribes and the white settlers and traders. They were noted for being fierce warriors and also, cunning entrepreneurs. For example, when one group of warriors from another tribe would use the Cree as a mediator, the Cree would charge 30 skins for two guns when the fur-trade post would only require 20 skins for two guns. The Cree were not only middle men between the tribes and white settlers, but also between other tribes. For some tribes, the distances were too far to travel to some of the fur-trading posts. As it was not safe to pass through traditional enemies' land, they went through the Cree "businessmen".

The history of how the Bible actually came to the native people is very interesting. Norman Taylor in his book, "My book, My people, Our Kingdom" gives some real insight as to how this happened and how the ancient prophecy was fulfilled for his people. (Because of time I won't directly quote his book but rather paraphrase what was given.) During this time of fur-trading at one of the posts, Natives noticed many white settlers walking into a huge building and saw that some were carrying a black book. They went to the building and peeked in through the windows to see what was going on. They saw people sitting in rows all facing one direction while a man spoke to them while holding a black book. "Could this be the book that is supposed to come to us?" Soon, word about the black book got out among many other tribes.[9]

One particular keynote speaker on the Christian history of the Cree related that one of the tribal groups took the initiative and told one of the Cree traders that they would not trade with the white settlers anymore if they did not send the man with the black book to them to show them the Way of Life[10]. The Cree were not the only ones who felt this way; other tribes such as the Ojibway and Salteaux also wanted the black book and if the Hudson's Bay officials did not bring the black book they would not bring any more furs[11]. Word then got out among the white traders about this message. Desperate, the Hudson Bay Company went to the Anglican, United and Roman Catholic churches, and other denominations requesting that they send priests with the black book (the Bible) so they could carry on their business with the Natives[12].

Others, who were not part of these negotiations, felt it was time to go to the tribes. Some were already on their way before the conditions between the Natives and fur-traders were set. One particular missionary ventured out on his own knowing that it could cost him his life; he knew that to come upon one of the tribal villages unannounced and uninvited meant to them that you were an invader, a spy and an enemy. Knowing this, he still went, trusting in God. He went un-armed, no extra coat, no food, no survival knife; all he had was his black Bible because he felt God wanted him to take only his black Bible with him. His journey was long and difficult. He traveled by canoe and dog sled. When he arrived in a particular village, the people naturally were alarmed and immediately attacked him, for they saw him as an intruder. As the crowd beat him over and over again, his black Bible fell out of his coat and a leader of the tribe saw it. Afraid of the book, the people did not kill him; neither did they destroy the book. Eventually, the people wanted to hear the Words of Life from the book[13]. This man, among many others, lived among indigenous people and shared with them the Words of Life from God's Holy Word, the Bible.

The previous account is similar to an event that took place among the Cree. They too, wanted the words that were written in the black book, later known as the Bible. God used the Cree tribe to open the door for other missionaries to share the Gospel of Christ among many other tribes. Another missionary

(James Evans), wanted the Cree to have the Word of God in their own language, so he prayed and God gave him inspiration. He invented what is known today as the Cree syllabic system which is the basis of our Cree language education in today's schools. He used this system to translate the Bible into Cree. He then taught our ancestors to read the syllabics and eventually our ancestors learned to read the Bible in their Native tongue. [14]

The Gospel of Christ was gladly received by our ancestors. Unfortunately, through time, things got ugly between the white officials and our people due to conflict over land and resources. Here you see Satan's work. As has been repeated orally, the Government sent out an order that all Native children be sent to residential schools run by various denominational churches, many of which had come at the request of the Hudson Bay Company fur traders. In these schools native children would learn English and religion and become "civilized". Not that they weren't already a civilized people, but they were viewed as savages by the dominant culture. So for three to five generations everywhere in Canada, many Native children were shipped or flown out and sent to residential schools far away from their homes, families and people. I know of Native people today in their late 50's and 60's who have shared with me how it happened for them. One of them related that when he was a child playing by a lake near their village, a strange looking thing, shaped like a bird, flew down and landed on the shores of the lake where he was. Then a man came out from the plane and gave him some good tasting food and invited him to look inside their plane. As he jumped in, the pilot also got in and soon they were in the air for a long time. When they landed, they were not at his homeland but in a strange country he had not seen before. From the plane he was taken to the nearest residential school and did not see his family again. Today, we hear one horror story after another of the many traumatic events that have taken place in the lives of the people who were sent to these residential schools.

In this unfortunate history of injustices I have come to see a similarity with the historical[15] and Biblical[16] accounts of the Hebrew children[17]. You read about it through the books of the Kings and the books of the prophets such as Daniel, Jeremiah, Ezekiel and others[18]. Time and time again, when the Hebrew children turned away from God, His judgment came upon them and they would go into captivity under another ruling nation. One particular time they were taken over by the King of Babylon[19], the dominant culture of that time. Hebrew children who were "*in the flower of their age*" (as Josephus called it), were to be enrolled in the institutes of Babylon, where they learned the Chaldean language, custom and laws[20]. The book of Daniel also speaks of Shadrach, Meshach, and Abed-nego; whose names respectively were Hananiah, Mishael and Asariah (see Daniel 1:6, 7). They also were some of those children. They found great favor in the political realm of the dominant nation of that day (see Daniel 1:19-20). Daniel was also one of those children and in him was found an excellent spirit (see Daniel 6:3). He played a key role in the courts of the King. No doubt some of the Hebrew children were viewed as scum and treated as such. No doubt they, too, had horrific experiences as they were taken and kept as captives for 70 years. Many of them had also witnessed the death of their parents and loved ones. As well, many of them became slaves to the Chaldean people. Yet, God, in the midst of this and in similar situations, rose up men and women from the Hebrew people as key leaders to act in their favor. Two such people are Daniel,[21] as mentioned earlier and later Esther[22], among many others. We can take great comfort from the lives of these people, who in the middle of captivity and difficult times, relied on God and saw His hand move on behalf of their people.

Therefore, in making this parallel, I see a pattern which has been re-enacted many times in history throughout the world. One nation dominates another and imposes their culture upon them. This pattern continues on to this day. Jesus prophesied that *"nation will rise against nation"* (see Matthew 24:7). When you study the word *nation* from the Greek text you find that it comes from the word *"ethnos"*[23] which is where we get the word *"ethnic"*[24]. What has happened in the history of our people and how our people were mistreated was not a unique occurrence, yet the injustice that occurred was not God's will for His creation whom He loves. I believe, however, that God has and will allow the nations, including our native nations, to be dominated even as He allowed the Jewish people to be dominated by Babylonians. God's plan and His desire is for true freedom which comes from Him (Exodus 3:7, 8; Daniel 7:27). Freedom from the Babylonians came as they turned to God; God intervened and the Babylonian regime was taken over by the Medes and Persians[25]. God moved King Artaxerxes' heart in favor towards the children of Israel so they were allowed to return to their homeland, to rebuild their temple and to worship the one true God[26]. When Jesus walked on the face of the earth, the people were under the regime of Rome. He came to offer a freedom that superseded any earthly domination (see John 8:32). **Only He can truly set people free, break the need to dominate, and heal the effects of being dominated**. This happens as people and nations turn to Him with all their hearts, for Jesus paid the price for our freedom with His Blood.

Considering the grief our people have gone through, the saddest thing is that many of their hearts became closed to the Gospel of Christ. *Can you blame them*? Too many tragic things had happened in the name of Christ. I was in the same boat years ago. My heart was hard and bitter towards Christianity, as at that time, I, like many of my people, did not realize there was a difference between religion and having a relationship with Jesus. If Christ had truly been the center of what was said to be Christianity, then none of these grievances would have occurred. What happened in the residential schools was not Christianity! It was men and women whose minds were filled with lust, perversion and legalism. Unless they have repented they will be held accountable to God for their crimes, whether here on earth or on the judgment day. Through it all, God is bigger than the devil and He is bigger than mankind's injustice. He is bigger than our unforgiveness and our hardness of heart; Jesus came to heal and set people truly free (see Isaiah 53).

We can practice all the cultural traditions and can learn every vowel and sound of our language (as valuable as our language is), yet still find that something is missing. What is the true solution? More money? Another written apology from the clergy or one more from the government? More sweat-lodges and more medicine men? More sage and sweet-grass? More cultural awareness weeks and healing circles? Let's face it; these things haven't worked.

The answer is to forgive.

It is impossible to truly forgive *outside of Christ.* He paid the ultimate price for our sins. He set the ultimate example for us. He was bruised and battered as though He were a beast; He was humiliated; *His rights taken away*; yet, He forgave all and in His greatest hour of pain, He prayed for those who pierced His hands and feet. You say that was 2000 years ago, what does that have to do with me today? It has everything to do with you and me also! Why did Christ suffer a horrible death on the cross of Calvary? He died for one sole purpose. What was His sole purpose in dying on the Cross?

Sin!

He died to pay the penalty for sin, to forgive and to cleanse the sin of the whole world. Whether we receive the forgiveness and cleansing of sin Christ died for, is up to us as individuals. He died for my sin. He died for the sins done to me. He died for those who sinned against me. He died for those I've sinned against. Sin. From before His time on earth to this very day, He was and is the Lamb of God, the Final Sacrifice. The wages of sin is death, but the gift of God is eternal Life. That gift is His Son, Jesus, sent into this world to reveal the Father and to die for our sins.

This real issue at hand is sin.

When we realize that we are in need of forgiveness, then we understand that we need Christ to come into our hearts, to cleanse us from all sin, including the sin of unforgiveness. Without forgiveness it is impossible to heal. When I finally surrendered my life to God, I wondered why I had been fighting Him. What a relief it was to ask Him to enable me to forgive the numerous ones who abused me and misrepresented Him in my life. You may be willing to forgive; yet, it seems you are not able to do this. His strength will give you the power to do it. I thank God that because of His grace, many of my people (including myself) have become resolved to forgive. I heard a native elder say, "It was never our land in the first place. It belonged to God. We need to forgive the white man and move on."

The true resolution to the problems stemming from past issues for our people, or any other people group, is to lay hold of what was accomplished at the cross where Christ died for the sins of the whole world. Culture cannot do this for us. Each of us must take our burdens to the cross and leave them with the Lord. We must allow ourselves to heal once and for all, and to embrace the cross and to follow His way. Outside of Christ, all is meaningless; but with Christ, the path shines brighter each day as we follow Him and His ways.

Over and over He sends His people out with the good news of the Gospel of Christ. He desires that all people come to know Him and to walk in His ways. Jesus truly is the Way, the Truth and the Life; there *is* no other way to the Father but through Him (John 14:6). All you have to do is believe in God's Son and accept Him into your heart as your Lord and Savior. Begin to seek His way and to walk in it. *Seek Him*, not other things. No one is more passionate about your soul than He is!

Christianity was never a white man's gospel, even though God used the white man to bring the gospel to the Native people. There are many white people who are still a heathen people. The Europeans did not have the Bible in their language until later in the Middle Ages. There were men, who were brave enough to challenge the controlling religious powers of their day. They began to translate God's Word from the original language to their Native tongue, so that all could read God's word and could come to know Him personally. Although men were burned at the stake for doing so, freedom began to come, and the way people thought and acted began to change. These changes birthed the reformation in all of Europe. The translation of the Bible into the common language of the people was a catalyst for change, in both the political and the religious realms of Europe. The Gospel then began to spread like wild fire among many European countries. God, in His sovereignty, was at work ensuring that His message to the world would be heard. The middle ages (also known as the "dark ages") came to an end. Many came into the freedom of knowing Christ. Some of these people came to our continent with a burning desire for others in far away lands to hear the Gospel of Christ. The Gospel of Christ is God's story to mankind about how everything began, what went wrong and how the problems of the past, present and future can be resolved. *It is His message for every tribe and every tongue.* For those who believe, new life comes (I Corinthians 5:17); true healing also comes through Him. This is different from "religion" with its rules and regulations.

However, the questions are: "Will the gospel of Jesus Christ work for my people or do we need to add on a few, perhaps many, extras? If the gospel of Jesus itself is not enough, then how many "extras" do we need? Where do we get them?

As a people group, we have tried to find help through cultural means. As well, we have tried many programs, government treaties, money, settlements and "religion". These things still haven't brought healing. Do we turn again, as many are encouraging us to do, to the accoutrements of our culture and to the wisdom of the medicine men and then add this to the gospel, or is the gospel of Jesus Christ alone enough to meet our needs? As we look for answers to the problems stemming from our past and present circumstances, these are indeed important questions which must be addressed as we continue on our journey.

PART THREE

CULTURAL IDENTIY IN CHRIST

– Why are we having an identity crisis?

I) *A SPIRITUAL JOURNEY.*

What does cultural identity have to do with our position in Christ?

The above question is a common one, being discussed today within the Body of Christ at large in light of cultural identity. I, for one, have grappled with this since the beginning of my walk with Christ. As a native woman, I have come face to face with this issue and have, in the past, walked down two differing paths which did not answer the heart of the question for me at all. During this time, it was as though an identity crisis would take me on a "tail spin" and soon I would be off to find who I was as a Native Christian. It was a journey that was going nowhere fast! I had many questions and I wanted to know: "What is the heart of the matter regarding cultural identity? "What does it have to do with our position in Christ?" After many years of pondering and searching for this answer, I have come to find in the Word of God the answer: cultural identity has nothing to do with our position in Christ. As Galatians 3:28 states, *"There is neither Jew nor Greek...for ye are all one in Christ Jesus."* Although this seems like an absolute conclusion, I believe the Word of God is very clear and absolute in light of the Blood of Christ, which was shed for the sins of the world, resulting in the restoration of our true identity - of who we really are in Christ,

(see II Corinthians 5:17).

In my search for truth and enrichment in my spiritual journey, I decided to put aside my cultural heritage and point of view regarding redemption of Native culture, as well as other people's opinions and interpretations of scripture. I decided to let the Word of God to me speak for itself. In so doing, I have come to understand some fascinating truths. Truly, the Word of God does not fail.

The human race is on a spiritual journey. We are searching for our reasons to exist, our purpose, and our destiny. *"What is the meaning to life and how can I find it?"* It seems almost everyone reflects on this question at some point in his or her life. We can look at this world and be amazed at how many different religions and cultures there are. Many are looking for fulfillment and inner peace with themselves and with

God. God made us, and God made all the different nations, but one thing He did not produce was what we call "religion". Often we put culture and religion in the same category. Usually one is closely identified with the other, but is God a religious God? No, He is not. He is a Holy God, and therefore, He does not need religion. What, then, is religion?

Inherently, man knows that he is sinful and is need of purification. Also, man knows deep within that there is a God, an ultimate Creator. For many, at some point in each one's life there begins a journey for fulfillment that can be found only by finding peace with God. *Religion is a system of works created by man to try and reach God.* It is a path devised by man to find peace with God. Religion encompasses various practices and ceremonies rooted in tradition. However, since these traditions were established by man, they are ineffective in reaching God. No matter how much man practices his religion, he ends up feeling empty and dissatisfied. There is no inner peace. Unless God intervenes and reveals His ways to us, we are lost. When He does this, we have an encounter with the living God and we personally receive Jesus as our Lord and Savior. We are changed from the inside out, not by rituals, but by God! Rather than just practicing a "religion", we are changed and we have a whole new way of life. Others may term it as "religion", but this way of living is the outcome of encountering God and being changed by Him, not ourselves. *Religion is practiced, whereas a life changing encounter with Jesus is experienced. The result is a new life in Him* (See II Cor.5:17).

Is God a cultural God? No, He is not. He is above culture, and therefore, He does not need culture. Man creates culture to meet sociological needs. *Culture then, is similar to religion in that it also is a man-made system.* It encompasses language, tradition, ideas, habits of living, beliefs, customs, art forms, rituals and ceremonies and this can also be incorporated within religion. Culture plays a major role in people's make up regarding who they are perceived and perceive themselves to be, as well as their attitudes, their values and their beliefs; this influence has a major role in their social life, their religious life, and the environment around them. This applies to the individual, as well as to the people group (or tribe). Naturally, this cultural depiction is passed down to succeeding generations.

Syncretism is as a blending of two religions. In this book, we are looking at syncretism in context of Christianity and other religions. Mankind often blends his own man-made religion and cultural components with Christian worship, attempting to blend both in order to create a meaningful spiritual experience. Syncretism is often unclear in what it actually believes (further in this book we will look into the heart of this issue).

As mentioned earlier, man creates culture to fill a need. It began in Eden with the fall of man when Adam and Eve disobeyed God's command to not eat the fruit of the tree of knowledge of good and evil. At that time, they became spiritually dead. The personal relationship that they once had with God was broken and they no longer communicated directly with Him (see Genesis 3). Because Adam and Eve were the first of the human race, the effect of their disobedience has tainted all subsequent humanity. This is where man first became lost, without peace, and without God (see Romans 5:12-16).

God, however, provided a way for man to reach Him! He sent His son Jesus to take man's sins by dying on the cross at Calvary. Jesus took upon Himself the punishment man deserves, namely, death. Because Jesus did this, we can be redeemed and spend eternity with God, rather than without God
(see Romans 5:17-21).

Jesus said, "*I am the way, the truth and the life: no man cometh to the Father, but by me*" (John 14:6). Our only access to God, the Creator, is through Jesus; we gain access to God by receiving Jesus as our personal Lord and Savior (see John 1:12, 13). Only through Him can we find the fulfillment of our spiritual journey. Peace and fulfillment are found in a personal relationship with Jesus.

"How do I as a Native person, relate to God and how does Christianity relate to me?"

This is a common question asked by many native people. Before a person can believe or personally relate to God as Lord, as King, as Father, and as Savior, a person must recognize that they are in need of God. As we begin to realize our need of God, then the desire for relationship with Him begins to grow. We begin to reach out to Him. Often we have questions regarding this relationship with God and how, or if, it can be developed in the context of our culture and what we have seen as "Christianity".

As these questions begin to arise, we often find ourselves not only dealing with this issue itself, but also, some cultural issues concerning how we as Native people often see ourselves in terms of the loss and redemption of our identity, our syncretism, and our beliefs and our values. Although these are complex issues, I want to endeavor to address them in this book.

Why are we Christians?

If there is anything I have learned in life so far it is this: *You cannot make a difference unless the difference is made in you.* For those of us who are Christians, it is important to ask: **Why are we Christians?** Why *do* we live a godly lifestyle? Is it because of our love for Jesus? Is it because it is "fire insurance" against spending eternity in Hell? Could it be the "call of God"? We become Christians because of what Jesus accomplished for us on the cross. "*Now that we have been made right with God by putting our trust in Him, we have peace with Him. It is because of what our Lord Jesus Christ did for us.*" (Romans 5:1, New Life Version). We were dying spiritually, desperately needing a Savior. Because of Christ we can live (see John 10:10). Christ came to restore to us our true identity. We all need to know WHO we are. The trouble today is that we are looking for earthly remedies to cure spiritual problems. I am not talking about alcohol, peer pressure, fame or fortune,

destructive as they are. I am talking about the human wisdom that is foolishness to God
(see I Corinthians 1:18-21).

We often devise carnal answers to the question of identity and then try to put a spiritual connotation on it by saying "God is restoring and redeeming this part of my identity". Instead of putting away old things, we try to save them by saying God is redeeming them. We have misunderstood that we have been consecrated by a new and living way through the blood of Christ (see Hebrew 10:19-20) and that old things are passed away (see II Cor.5:17).

If God thought that redeeming fleshly things would bring healing to us as a people, then what was the point of sending His son Jesus to die on the cross? Did Christ not say on the cross, "*It is finished*"?

Syncretism (which, in the context of this book, is the blending of another religion with Christian faith), does not line up with Biblical teaching. I believe it is a devilish doctrine that has crept into the church today, and unfortunately, many Christians (both non-Native and Native) are buying into it. Christian Natives, who are opposed to the idea of redeeming native culture, call syncretism "mixing". This helps to bring an exact and simple understanding of what syncretism is.

Colossians 2:8 "*See to it that no one carries you off as spoil or makes you yourselves captive by his so-called **philosophy and intellectualism** and vain deceit (idle fancies and plain nonsense), following human tradition* *(**men's ideas of the material** rather than the spiritual world), just crude notions following the rudimentary and elemental teachings of the universe and disregarding [the teachings of] Christ (the Messiah)*" The Amplified Bible[27] (emphasis mine)

II) *THE CRISIS*

Earlier in this book I mentioned some of the many injustices that my people suffered. I personally know the struggle, the despair, the devastation and the loss. Many of my generation of Native people really do not have much to look forward to in life. They are suffering the consequences that the older generation sowed because of their own wounds from the past. Our parents were not healed enough themselves to raise the next generation to survive in the world. Think about it. The First Nations people who once were strong and proud have been dominated and have had their land taken over, treaties signed and broken. They were treated like animals and put on reservations to be isolated from the rest of society. In the name of law and order native children were taken from their homes and put into residential schools where they learned "proper education and religion". Many of these schools are guilty of having done more harm than good as evidenced by the millions of dollars the Government of Canada is giving out to those natives who were forced into the residential schools across Canada. When you listen to the testimonies of the generations that were in those schools, you can feel their pain as they share the horrors they faced. These are the parents of many native children who are now between ages 15-40. Craig Smith writes,

"The end result of the boarding school experience was a generation of native people who were stripped of their identity, and told that everything about them was bad. They were told nothing is worthwhile or salvageable in their culture and if they were to survive, they were to adapt to the ways of the dominate society. Most Native children who came out of that tragic time in our history were not willing or able to adapt their ways to that of the dominate society. So when a people are led to believe their culture is bad, and they resolutely refuse to adapt to another's culture they end up being a people with no culture or identity"[28]

Because of these injustices, there was a real sense of a loss of identity among native people. What we are experiencing now, over the last few decades, is a renewed search for that lost identity. In searching for their identity, natives are reaching back to the traditions of their ancestors. You can't blame them. But has it helped them any? As far as I have witnessed, I conclude the answer as "no". It has only taken them down a path of greater darkness and confusion. Native people are on a soul search. They are having an identity crisis, but have not successfully resolved it. The Body of Christ has done little to bring healing so far. Although other races are not excluded, it would appear that God has reserved the majority of that work for the Native Christians who are now rising up in God to reach their own people. Native Christians can identify with Native problems. They know the struggles and the conflicts. However, if they are going to truly help their people to have a new life in Jesus, they must also know the Healer and the Deliverer and the biblical answer to the identity crisis and the confusing questions of syncretism or "mixing".

The search for identity is not just a native issue; it is an issue for all mankind in general. God has brought me to a place where I now realize that I do not need sacraments, substances, customs, traditions, or special events to find my healing and my identity. I have come to realize that no matter what I do or where I go or how far I get in life, the thing that matters most is: DO I KNOW JESUS AS MY PERSONAL LORD AND SAVIOUR? Have I accepted what He has done for me and IS WHAT HE HAS DONE GOOD ENOUGH or DO I NEED SOMETHING ELSE?

> Galatians 4:8-9, "*But at the previous time, when you had not come to be acquainted with and understand and know the true God, you [Gentiles] were in bondage to gods who by their very nature could not be gods at all [gods that really did not exist]. Now, however, that you have come to be acquainted with*

and understand and know [the true] God, or rather to be understood and known by God, how can you turn back again to the weak and beggarly and worthless elementary things [of all religions before Christ came], whose slaves you once more want to become?" The Amplified Bible [29] (emphasis mine).

III) *IDENTITY IN CULTURE*

In my own native upbringing, I was taught that culture is simply a way of life conforming to the traditions, customs and religion of our family, community and tribe. One author gives this insight regarding the concept of culture:

"Culture is that complex whole which includes knowledge, belief, art, morals, law, custom, and any other capabilities and habits acquired by man as a member of society"[30]

As such, culture is linked to our identity as individuals or as a people group. The role of identification is significant within a group setting of a society for those individuals belonging to that particular group. In my travels between numerous Native tribal groups within Canada and the U.S.A., I find distinct and unique characteristics within each group of tribal peoples I visit. Not all hold the same values and beliefs regarding the make up of their culture and religion, for each tribal group has developed their own distinct culture. Since cultures differ from one group to another, it is clear that within each community, among the tribal groups, an individual's sense of identity will vary according to which particular community/tribal group one belongs to.

First of all, I was born into the Cree tribe. Among the Cree, there are specific elements that identify us as Cree. For example: our language is Cree. Other tribal groups have their own language and cannot communicate with another tribe unless there is an interpreter who knows the language of the other group or a common language, such as English, is used. Not only is our native language unique but the patterns and design used to make moccasins are also distinctly unique between tribal groups. The Cree have the toe part of the moccasin in a rounded shape; whereas, the Blackfoot will have their toes more pointed. The tribal groups of the north use fur around the ankle to keep snow from getting inside their footwear, but the southern tribes don't. The Cree use a moss bag to carry their new born babies; the Northern Tuchone` shape a large piece of birch bark to carry the baby; the Inuit use what they call "amautik", which is cloth material or Caribou hide made into a back pouch to carry their babies in. The Cree do not carve totem poles; although the coastal tribes of the west do. The Cree, among other plains Indian tribes, will have round dances to rally the community for gatherings for special occasions; whereas, most of the Métis and Northern tribes will have what they call Tea Dances. The Cree, among other southern tribes, will often have pow-wows, but many northern tribes will have what they identify as drum dances and "feeding the fire" ceremonies. The coastal tribes of the west will have what they call potlatches. These few examples demonstrate the diversity between tribal groups.

The uniqueness and diversity of each tribal group is important to consider when reviewing the trage-dies of the residential school system. Within these schools, every aspect of our identity regarding the unique cultural aspects of our Native people was stripped away, resulting in a loss of our identity. Although some have managed to maintain or regain the old cultural practices, still others have steered down a path of hopelessness. I have seen many of my people trying to ease their pain through alco-holism and drug addiction; yet, they end up dying in their pain and addiction. I have also witnessed others take steps of recovery and begin to "search for their roots" in order to find who they are on their spiri-tual journey. On the other hand, I have seen many others come to know Christ as their personal Lord and Savior and discover the true meaning of life and what it is to walk with God according to His ways as they find healing in Christ.

When we become followers of Jesus, we do not change cultures; however, we do acquire a new iden-tity and, because of this, our behavior will change within the context of our culture. Following the one true God *does not make us any more or less Native than we already are.* If we are born Native, biologi-cally, that cannot be changed. We do not have to live in a Native community nor do we have to practice the old traditions and rituals to prove that we are Native. It is our corporate heritage. We are born Native and

Native we remain. Regardless of whether we are Christian or non-Christian, we are Native people. However our "identity" is more of an individual thing; it has to do with how we define ourselves individually. I can define myself as a Native Christian. My personal identity is in Christ, but I still physically belong to a certain people group: I am Native. However, my identity is not complete without Christ.

Another way of looking at the difference between culture and identity is to see that culture consist of structures, ways of thinking, and ways of behavior. Traditional belief systems, developed within a people group, give that people a sense of a cooperate identity, thus enabling them to survive. When Christ comes into our lives He begins to infiltrate every aspect of who we are as people. On the other hand, those things that do not conform to Him are of no lasting value. One author put it this way: *"We were dead in trespasses and sins. We had learned to live a life independent of God. Our identity and perception of ourselves were formed and programmed into our minds through the natural orders of this world."*[31] **Apart from Christ our identity is like the hand without the glove.**

IV) *OUR TRUE IDENTITY*

In light of "going back to our roots" let us go back further than ten or twenty generations to the first man (Adam) and the first woman (Eve). John R. Cross in his book "Stranger on the Road to Emmaus", shares this amazing discovery by scientists "...*studies of human DNA conclude that we all have one man and one woman in our ancestry.*"[32] Let's now proceed to God's Word. Genesis 1:**26**, states that God made man in His image. Further in Genesis 3 we read the account of the fall of man, which is where the corruption of our identity began.

"*Now the serpent was more subtle than any beast of the field which the Lord God had made. And he said unto the woman, Yea, hath God said, Ye shall not eat of the fruit of every tree of the garden?' And the woman said unto the serpent, We may eat of the fruit of the trees of the garden: But of the fruit of the tree which is in the midst of the garden, God hath said, Ye shall not eat of it, neither shall ye touch it, lest ye die. And the serpent said unto the woman, Ye shall not surely die: For God doth know that in the day ye eat thereof, then your eyes shall be opened, and ye shall be as gods, knowing good and evil. And when the woman* <u>saw</u> *that the tree was good for* <u>food</u>*, and that it was pleasing to the* <u>eyes</u>*, and a tree to be desired to make one* <u>wise</u>*, she took of the fruit thereof, and did eat, and gave also unto her husband with her; and he did eat. And the eyes of them both were opened, and they both knew that they were naked; and* <u>they sewed fig leaves together, and made themselves aprons.</u> *And they heard the voice of the Lord God walking in the garden in the cool of the* *day: Adam and his wife hid themselves from the presence of the Lord God amongst the trees of the garden.*"(Genesis 3:1-8, emphasis added).

Adam and Eve's act of disobedience resulted in spiritual separation from God and the spiritual death of their relationship with Him. Not only were Adam and Eve spiritually separated from God, but their identity and how they saw themselves also changed. They no longer saw themselves in the likeness of God. They now saw themselves as separate from God and saw their nakedness without Him. For the first time, they experienced shame. The significance of sewing fig leaves together to make themselves aprons cannot be ignored. Covering was not necessary at one time. Before this incident they were completely un-ashamed of their nakedness, for God Himself was their covering. After they disobeyed God, His covering was removed and they ran in fear to find something else to cover their shame; this led to actually trying to hide from the presence of the Lord. Although their physical nakedness was covered, it did not change how they really felt inside because they had acquired a sin nature. Through Adam all of humanity became corrupted by sin (see Romans 5:12).

Man-kind's culture became a counterfeit identity by replacing our true identity which had been stripped away and taken over by Satan, the father of lies, as he usurped the dominion over earth that had originally been given to Adam and Eve. Why are so many native people having such an identity crisis? It is because: a) they have no idea of their true identity in God and b) their man-made identity, as expressed through their culture, has been stripped way from them through the residential school system which left them feeling "naked". Culture cannot replace the inward emptiness that mankind inherently feels.

God, however, made a solution for man to come to Him His way! "*Unto Adam also and to his wife did the Lord God make coats of skins, and clothed them*" (Genesis 3:21). In this account, for the first time, man saw blood that was shed sacrificially and saw death. John R. Cross put it this way:

> "This was a graphic illustration of the fact that sin brings death. Adam and Eve had never seen death before. If they watched, it must have been a jarring experience – seeing the blood spilled on the ground, the grasping for life, the shine pass from the animal's eye, comprehending the finality. Whatever the case, God made the awful reality of death understandable to them immediately. Animals died in order that they might be clothed."[33]

God made death a very vivid reality. Shedding blood, thus covering them with the skin of the animals was a way of atonement for Adam and Eve's sin. Their sin was temporarily covered by God. Further on in Genesis 4, Cain and Abel both made sacrifices to the Lord. We read how Abel made the more acceptable sacrifice by offering the firstling of his flock and the fat. We can assume that this practice of offering the sacrifice of a lamb was an oral tradition taught by their parents, Adam and Eve. We do know it was what God wanted as evidenced by God's response to Able and confirmed later by what was written in the scriptures (Leviticus 1:2-9). This offering pointed them to the true Lamb that God would send to not only cover sin, but rather take it away. Christ came as the Lamb of God. When John the Baptist saw Jesus coming, he shouted, "...*Behold the Lamb of God, which taketh away the sin of the world*" (John 1:29). Christ came to redeem all of humanity from corruption and spiritual separation from our Heavenly Father. As we yield to His authority, we come to the place where we repent and believe the gospel (which means to turn around and believe the good news). We accept what He has done for us and His Spirit begins to work in us. He restores our original state of unity with God. We no longer have to walk in shame, for we are covered by Him. In fact, when we become "born again" we become partakers of the very nature of God; we become part of God's family; we become a new creation.

For the believer THERE IS NO TRUE IDENTITY OUTSIDE OF CHRIST. Without Christ our culture, our world-view and our way of thinking is twisted and perverted by the god of this world so that we are kept from the truth of dependence on God for everything, including our identity.

As we continue looking at our true identity, John 4:23-24, states: "*But the hour cometh, and now is, when the true worshippers shall worship the Father in spirit and in truth: for the Father seeketh such to worship him. God is a Spirit: and they that worship him must worship him in Spirit and in truth.*" God, our Creator, is a Spirit and He created us in His image. Therefore we are spirits living in a fleshly body. When we are born again we become a new creation. We are native in the flesh, but in the spirit we became His sons and daughters when we accepted Christ as the One who paid the price for our sins. II Corinthians 5:17 states: *"Therefore if any man be in Christ, he is a **new creature**: old things are passed away; behold all things are become new.*" (emphases added). Not only are we new creatures; we also, as God's adopted sons and daughters, begin a new way of life. We have God's Spirit abiding in us and His ways must become our ways. We were lost before we came to the saving knowledge of Jesus, but now we are found; therefore, we begin to walk in a new way of life in Jesus. We are followers of Christ (not a religious system) and now identify ourselves with Christ. We call ourselves Christians because we find our identity in Him. How we used to identify ourselves no longer applies. Neil T. Anderson states:

> "When asked to describe themselves, people usually mention race, religion, cultural background or social distinction....Paul said none of these apply anymore, because our identity is no longer determined by our physical heritage, social standing or racial distinctions. Our identity lies in the fact that we are all children of God and we are in Christ".[34]

When we realize where our true identity rests, it becomes very meaningful to say, "*I am a Christian*". I talk, breath, sing, walk, live and worship as a child of God, not just as a native person. Being Native does not make me more special than any one else. God's Word says that "He is no respecter of persons, but accepts men from every nation when they turn to Him" (see Acts 10:34-35). The word *nation* in this context of scripture originates from the Greek word: "*ethnos*"[35], which is where we get the word "*ethnic*"[36]. In this passage of Scripture, it is clear that this word refers to all racial groups. We are all equal in the eyes of God.

The God I am talking about is not a "*white man's god*", but the God who is completely Sovereign over all mankind; the God who is omnipresent (meaning that He is everywhere at all times); the God who is omnipotent (meaning He is all-powerful); the God who is omniscient (meaning He is all-knowing). He is our Creator and because He is, we ought to heed His Word and to respect Him for WHO He is. This is how we relate to Him as Natives, as individuals, and as sons and daughters of God. Hebrew 11:6 states: "*But without faith it is impossible to please him: for he that cometh to God must believe that he is, and that he is a rewarder of them that diligently seek him.*" We look to Him and respond to Him as our Heavenly Father. We, therefore, should start to live as He requires and we should see ourselves as His sons and daughters. Ephesians 2:19-20, states: "*Now therefore ye are no more strangers and foreigners, but fellow citizens with the saints, and of the house-*

hold of God; and are built upon the foundation of the apostles and prophets, Jesus Christ Himself being the Chief Cornerstone;".

If culture was not created by God, but by man, why then do we try to redeem it? Christ came to redeem **us** (as individuals), not our culture, and to conform **us** into **His** image. We have it backwards. It should not be culture changing our Christianity, but Christ changing our culture. God did not come to redeem our culture. He came to redeem the person. God does not need culture. He is above culture. Galatians 4:5, shows that Jesus came, "*To redeem them that were under the law* ..." (emphasis mine). The word law in this scripture also relates to the unwritten rules of culture.

V) *HIDDEN CULTURAL EXPECTATION AND RACISM*

Culture and racial distinction are often barriers which society must leap over. People often make distinctions about which racial background they belong to. I personally believe that doing this has the potential to lead to racism, pride, a superiority complex and giving offense to others. Our belief systems and values often develop into prejudices, not only against other people groups, but also against any individuals whose ideas, mannerisms and conduct is different from ours. For example, in North America, when greeting one another, it is common to shake hands. In another country, people may greet one another with a kiss. Can you imagine the clash there would be when the "hand greeter" meets the "kiss greeter"? A friend shared this story with me when she first began to work among the northern Cree of AB. She noticed that when shaking hands with them, how loosely they would grip the hand. At first, she found this odd and rather cold, until she came across a book by Thomas King, *"Medicine River"*. This helped her to understand this "hand-shaking" custom. The author illustrated that Native people feel that white people approach hand-shaking like a contact sport.[37] She laughed and realized that it wasn't a personal affront; it is just the way they shake hands as given in his book *"Medicine River"*.

Prejudice arises from assumed expectations. These expectations can be cultural or personal. When someone we encounter doesn't meet our expectations, we become offended. We withhold acceptance of that person who, in turn, feels rejected and may also become offended. The "offender" may not even realize how he has offended. This leads to mutual withdrawal, defensiveness, rejection, resentment, and contempt.

To be prejudiced is to have a biased opinion towards someone or something. Prejudice has a twin called racism. To be racist is think the race you come from is superior to other races. Racism is a concept man created, not God. One author put it this way:

"We make such a fuss over being different from one another, in skin color, in philosophy, in taste, and in religion. From the beginning, God did not make us different and His intention was for us to be alike in every way. 'Let us make man in our image'(Genesis 1:26). God the Father, God the Son and God the Holy Spirit are alike in every way. They have different responsibilities, but they function in unity as one. We, as God's children, should function in unity in the same way. We have different responsibilities in our work for the Lord, but that does not make us different as far as our likeness to Him. God has never been concerned with race, skin color or ethnic pride. Instead, God's problem with man from the very beginning was unrighteousness and a lack of holiness"[38]

Romans 12:3b states: "...*to every man that is among you, not to think of himself more highly than he ought to think; but to think soberly, according as God hath dealt to every man the measure of faith.*" We need HUMILITY in our relations with one another.

Often we think we are culturally justified by God to hold offenses. For example, we find it hard to forgive racism. However, God's answer to us is to forgive. What did Jesus say on the cross? He said, "*Father, forgive them; for they know not what they do...*" (Luke 23:34)

Our society has tried to combat racism and prejudice by promoting the values of tolerance, peace and harmony between other people and cultures. However, we have failed to address the root of the problem. We are to be one in Jesus Christ. Often it seems that celebrating the diversity of culture creates more racism than unity and harmony. Racism and prejudice are like dandelions. You cut off the top, but a day later the dandelion grows back. It is not until you dig out the root that you truly get rid of it. I heard a special speaker say it this way, "*Racism is not a skin problem, it is a sin problem.*"[39]

There is a great deal of talk about fighting racism; yet, nothing really seems to work in eliminating it regardless of what culture it occurs in. Promoting unity, peace and harmony, has proven unsuccessful in eradicating the problem. What is the real answer?

Part of the solution lies in forgiveness, but forgiveness will not take place until one chooses to let go of one's pride. Pride is at the root of racial prejudice. It causes one to think oneself as better than the other. Racism means a thought or belief that one's own race and culture is superior to another race and culture.

I am an aboriginal. I am a Plains Cree, and I am not ashamed of my cultural and racial origin. However, I must guard against racial prejudice because there is the temptation for me to use my culture and racial origin as an excuse for problems I encounter. In order to guard against this, I must cast down my pride and take it to the cross, daily. As God's child I am to walk in the same manner as Jesus did, that is, to walk humbly with my God. Philippians 2:5-8 states: "*Let this mind be in you, which also is in Christ Jesus: Who, being in the form of God, thought it not robbery to be equal with God: But made Himself of no reputation, and took upon Him the form of a servant, and was made in the likeness of men: And being found in the fashion as a man, he humbled himself, and became obedient unto death, even the death of the cross.*"

I have been in some Native communities belonging to tribes other than the Cree. As soon as some of the people heard that I was Cree, they would say, "*The Cree came over our mountains and slaughtered our village and stole our women.*" My attitude was "*That was more than 200 year ago!*" Nevertheless, racism was still there. One time I stood up to face a young Native man who shouted this accusation at me and in a slightly joking manner, I replied, "*On behalf of the Cree, I'm very sorry.*" This humble answer stopped the criticism. People often live in the past and hold grudges. People like to think they are better than others. I have no right to say, "*The Cree are better than...*". That would be saying that God made me better than everyone else. Galatians 3:28 gives us another perspective regarding cultural and racial issues: "*There is neither Jew nor Greek, there is neither bond nor free, there is neither male nor female: for ye are all one in Christ Jesus.*" The only solution to racism is what Christ has done for us on the cross. It is possible for us to forgive. Accepting what Christ has done breaks down our pride and then God's love is shed abroad in our hearts (see Romans 5:5). Only the perfect love of God will cause us to see one another as one in Christ Jesus. I John 4:18 tells us that perfect love casts out all fear. In the case of cultural and racial issues, could this fear be the fear of being inferior to another culture and race? We must allow God's love to fill us and allow His love to cast out all fear.

If we do not apply the cross to racial prejudice in our personal lives, we will never resolve the issue. Ephesians 2:14-16 states, *"For He is our peace, who hath made both one, and hath broken down the middle wall of partition between us; having abolished in His flesh the enmity, even the law of commandments contained in ordinances; for to make in Himself of twain one new man, so making peace; And that He might reconcile both unto God in one body by the cross, having slain the enmity thereby."* We can apply these scriptures to racism in that this enmity (racism) has been destroyed at the cross - even the *"law of commandments contained in ordinances"*, which are the hidden cultural expectations of our people. We are only meant to live up to God's expectations. We must release others from our cultural expectations and allow them to live up to God's expectations. Christ broke down the middle wall of partition concerning our relationship with God and with each other. Rick Joyner gives the following insight:

> "The cross of Christ confronts and overcomes both the pride of man and his insecurity. The Holy Spirit was sent to the world to convict the world of sin, because it is the revelation of our sin that drives us to the cross to find grace and forgiveness. This destroys our pride by establishing our dependency on the Savior, which also restores our trust in Him. The deeper the cross works in us, the more humble we will become, and the more secure in His love. When we, who are so foreign to

God's nature, are accepted back into Him by grace, it works a tolerance in us for those who are different from our nature. Also, those who are becoming spiritual begin to judge from the spiritual perspective, not after the flesh."[40]

Christ bore our iniquities and our transgressions as explained in Isaiah 53:5, "*But He was wounded for our transgressions, he was bruised for our iniquities: the chastisement of our peace was upon him; and with his stripes we are healed.*" Christ took the punishment of both our sins against God and our sins against each other upon Himself. **The only real answer to being healed of our wounds is what Christ did on the cross for us**. We can be healed in our relationship with each other on the basis of the cross. This is wonderful news!

PART FOUR

SYNCRETISM – "MIXING"

Culture is often misunderstood. Culture relates to worship, religion, and tradition. How do you distinguish what is acceptable and what is not acceptable in the eyes of God? What we *do* must glorify *God* if we are to be fruitful in our Christian walk. Only the Spirit of God can make us fruitful vessels of His glory. *"And thou shalt swear, The Lord liveth, in truth, in judgment, and in righteousness; and the NATIONS shall bless themselves in him, and IN HIM SHALL THEY GLORY"* Jeremiah 4:2, (emphasis added). According to Jeremiah, the nations (all ethnic groups), shall glory *in God*; not in or through culture.

I) *TWO MISTAKES*

I find it quite interesting that today there is a renewed interest in the exaltation of ethnic cultures within the body of Christ. In our conferences, seminars and churches, we now accept and celebrate the diversities of cultures instead of simply celebrating and focusing on Jesus. Instead of a total spurning of those things which are not of God and are not produced by His Spirit, there is now great acceptance of them. This has opened the door for the deception of syncretism to creep in, often in the form of the performing arts or under the guise of "prophetic acts".

Not too long ago, there was total condemnation of Native culture. For example, there was a time when the Catholic Church (and others, as well) told natives not to have any thing to do with their culture. The government also supported this policy and allowed the church to take Native children off the reserves and place them in residential schools to educate them and to civilize them in the ways of the white society. The prevailing philosophy was that natives needed to be merged into the prevailing white society, religion and culture. Therefore in the residential schools, Native customs, traditions, religious beliefs and languages were rigorously suppressed. Natives were often told that their language was of the devil and that everything about them was devilish and needed to be cleansed. If any of the students spoke their language, they were severely punished. Sad to say, many students were physically, sexually, emotionally, and spiritually abused in these schools.

Today, these polices have been totally reversed. The denominations that formerly ran the residential schools now admit that there was widespread abuse in the residential school system. They have publicly apologized to native communities and many are now rushing to embrace native cultural traditions and even native religious beliefs. When native people mix their religious traditional cultural practices with Christian faith it is called syncretism. As native people, we often call it "mixing". David Sitton writes:

> *"To dispose of important cultural traits without replacing them leaves the people with a cultural void and more susceptible to syncretism in an effort to satisfy the unmet needs"*[41]

Two extremes have taken place. First, it was extreme legalism and now it is extreme compromise. The Catholic Church is not the only denomination that has seen this pendulum swing. There are many organizations that are following the same policies. Before we go on further, I want to make it clear that I do not condone the abuses of the residential schools, nor do I believe that our native languages, nor we as a people, are devilish. Neither do I support the preaching of condemnation towards cultures. That is what religion does. **As God's people, we are simply called to lift up Jesus,** nothing more and nothing less. Have we forgotten this simple principle which Jesus Himself laid out? (See John 12:32). The purpose of this book is for God's people to take a look at the matter of redeeming culture. Underlying the concept of redeeming culture is the question: *"Is Jesus enough and is what He did enough or do we need to add in something else?"* Most of the church today is afraid of offending Native people or feel badly for the abuse many natives suffered; so, instead of preaching truth and repentance, they are preaching redemption of native culture and are incorporating it into Christian worship. They are teaching only partial repentance. Since culture is man-made it often can lead to separation from God rather than drawing people to God. No wonder Jesus said in John 6:44(a) *"No man can come to me, except the Father which hath sent me draw him:..."* Culture cannot do this.

Many in the church and some streams of society have expressed feeling guilt and sorrow over the way native people were treated in the past. Consequently there is a movement to accept and to accommodate everything in native culture whether it is scripturally correct or not. Many people feel that to say no to anything native, would be perceived as rejecting the native people which is what they do not want to do. However, nowhere in Scripture have I found syncretism to be accepted. Redemption of native culture or any other culture is not the goal of the gospel. *Christ came to redeem the person not our cultural ways.*

Another problem is that it seems most Christian Natives are not able to fit in to the churches of the white culture. That concern is making native culture a focus in some of the churches at large in order to make a place for Christian Natives. On a personal note, thank you for your heart! However, let's continue to look at some of the issues.

As a young Christian, I attended a city church. After a couple of years one of the senior co-pastors commented how I had so changed, that I used to be so "native" and now God was doing a beautiful work. I did not know if I should take that as a compliment or as an insult because it seemed like her comment about being so "native" was a put down. I replied, saying, *"Yes. God is changing my character to become more like Him"*, but I left her office feeling confused about who I was as a Christian native person. I am not trying to be "white". I just wanted to be who God made me to be and to pursue Him, not to imitate another culture. Maybe she was referring to the way I used to dress. There was a time in my life when wearing leather jackets and black leather boots with an indigenous style was important to me. I loved to wear black leather biker jackets and other leather coats with fringes and beads and studs. It gave me some sense of glory and pride, and an image that I purposely portrayed. I was proving to the world and to the church that I was not religious, but rather, I was free. At this phase in my life, God was dealing with a root of rebellion that controlled my thoughts and attitudes in how I related with people. My eyes began to open one day. When stepping onto a transit bus in the city, I noticed a granny looking at me with fear, and taking a tight grip on her purse. This bothered me and I asked the Lord to search my heart. He showed me that with this "tough" image, I portrayed intimidation and that this was not Christ-like. If I was to be a minister of the Gospel, people needed to see Jesus, not the flesh. The image had to go! No white man told me this. It was the Lord opening my eyes. After repenting for living this way, I knew what I had to do in order to be rid of the stronghold of rebellion in my heart. I got rid of my black leather jacket. When I took it to the nearest pawn shop, all they gave me was $25. The Lord spoke to my heart in the pawn shop, *"That's how cheap that image is!"* That pastor probably related the way I dressed as being Native because of the style of my leather jacket which had fringes all over it. She did not know why I wore it, so her comment was innocent, in a sense. I was the one who made steps to change my "dress code", so to speak. This change was made not so that I could fit into a white cultured church, but to deal with an ungodly characteristic in my life.

Another white pastor has shared with me her concern about the white-cultured churches using fancy pink pews, seeker friendly services, bigger sound systems, "proper" dress code and speech, and the right style of music in order to attract more people. She commented that when this becomes a priority in our churches to bring people to God, that this type of cultural emphasis takes away from focusing on Jesus, even as does any other cultural emphasis. (If we in deed go to church to worship Jesus, then the emphasis must be on Him, not our cultural accoutrements). Native people are not the only group of people who feel awkward in these churches. There are even white people that do not attend these churches because they cannot fit into the form either. **People are hungry for Jesus!** They want to feed on His Word and experience His presence, not just cultural expressions of Christianity. The world can give them all the culture they want.

Let me relate two other experiences I had. The first was when I attended a church in Rocky Mountain House, Alberta. The non-Native pastor of this church at that time had previously ministered among native peoples. When he began to serve in this church, he started to change the order of the church services to a "Native-style", allowing room for testimonies and specials. It didn't seem to be working well and they went back into a more contemporary style of worship. Because I had been in and out of the community to travel, I could follow the progress of this change. On one occasion he had me speak on a Sunday and asked me to lead part of the song service in the way that I was accustomed to. I had never felt so awkward in my life. I could tell the people in the church felt awkward, too. After trying not to lose my compo- sure and to laugh because I felt nervous and caught between two cultural expressions of worship, I rushed through what I had to share and was glad when it was over. I've thought a great deal about that service. I knew that the pastor was honoring the "Native flow" and music to which I was accustomed; however, I'm sure he could feel the vibes in the service that day too - that it did not "work". Amazingly enough, this church still loves me and supports me as a traveling missionary in the north. I've often asked myself, *"What went wrong that day?"* Well, the obvious answer is that both cultures clashed. It would have been better for me to thank the pastor for wanting to give me the opportunity to sing and play before I preached, however, instead of me leading worship; he should have had their worship leader lead in the way they were accustomed to. That would have prevented the hindrance to the flow of God's Word while I preached.

(When I refer to Native style or flow, I do not mean beating on native drums or pow-wow dancing. Instead I am referring to the kind of music learned from the Tent Meetings and revivals that have come through native communities).

The second experience is with one of the couples that lead worship in that church, and who have also teamed up with our ministry team on occasion. This experience taught me a wonderful lesson of humility. This couple, are musicians in their own right. When they first came with me to one of the native communities in central B.C., I witnessed a beautiful act of grace. They did not insist that because they were already worship leaders in their church that they should be able to play the contemporary style of music and songs they knew. Instead, they made every effort to blend with the flow of the people. I had only two years experience playing the guitar and singing the songs that our Native people love to sing; yet, they co-operated with me as the worship leader. How very humbling. With this spirit of unity and humility, God's blessing was upon us and we experienced His wonderful presence with the people we ministered to.

The events which took place on that outreach with them taught me some principles for life and ministry. Sometimes we just have to lay aside our pre-conceived ideas or ways of doing things in order to co-operate with one another. As ministers of the gospel our purpose is to be a channel of blessing of God's grace and to love those that know Him and those that do not.

I believe that there are cultural customs that have a place in our churches, but they cannot take precedence over the Word of God and our focus on Him. When I say cultural customs I am not relating to religious cultural practices. I am relating to everyday life cultural practices. For example: In most Christian Native gatherings there will be a supper provided at the end of the service(s). The reason for the supper is that the host is concerned for those that have traveled long distances to get to the meeting and does not want to send them home hungry. The other reason is to honor the guest ministry speaker/team. This is a cultural practice that is not only among the Christian Natives, but also among non-Christian Native gatherings.

Another example in the same setting is that the Native Christians will have what they call "testimony time" when people are allowed to get up and to share what God has done for them and what He has laid on their hearts from the Word or to sing a song. This also is a practice of the Native people in general, where room is made for others to share before the main speaker speaks, whether in a church or in a community meeting.

One more other example: I was with a ministry team (many of us from different races), in a Native church in Prince Rupert, B.C. At the end of the service the people had our team line up at the front of the church in front of all the people. The local musicians played on their instruments and the one leading the protocol had all the people that were there that night come and shake our hands to bless us in the name of the Lord. Some hugged us and thanked us for coming to minister to them. This was a beautiful experience. I had experienced this before with this particular tribal group and it was touching to see how the ministry team I was with was so touched by the love expressed. The people then prayed a blessing over us as we departed on the next leg of our journey. This practice has been a custom of this people group for generations. Their intent was not to honor us but to thank God for sending us to them. At times, in some of the villages where we have been, people would come by the place where we were staying to give us some fish or some wild meat just to bless us. Some of these people never stepped into our meetings at all. There is nothing wrong with these types of cultural practices, so long as the customs do not take priority over the preaching of God's Word and our focusing on Him, which is the main purpose for which we gather in His Name. There is a proper balance!

When culture becomes our primary focus, then we as a church have missed the mark. Whether feathers and native drums or "pink pews" and seeker friendly services become a priority, it is then that we have lost sight of our purpose as to why we gather in His Name. If the Holy Spirit cannot draw the people in and to the Lord, then no culture of whatever group will do the job. If people are coming to church because of cultural accoutrements then the whole focus is wrong. Jesus did not die on the cross for our culture. If we are joined together on the basis of connecting with our culture then what is the purpose of meeting in His Name at all? The world is already doing just that. God did not intend for the church to be caught up in man's ways, methods, style or form in order to meet together. Rather, Christ died for our sin that we might be reconciled to God; and by being reconciled to Him, His presence is made manifest to us on the basis of the Blood of Jesus and our dependence on that alone.

I must clarify at this point that there are some concepts of Native religion hidden in the word "culture". Today the words "cultural" and "spiritual" are almost synonymous. However, a long time ago, "cultural" had a broader meaning. For example: *regalia* at one time were simply our everyday clothing. Today, however, regalia signify special clothing worn for rituals, initiations, pow-wows and specific religious ceremonies. (Regalia may or may not include some items like moccasins and mukluks, which are also used in place of slippers or for comfort for indoor/outdoor wear.) There are many things added to Cree Native culture today that were never practiced nor believed traditionally. An example of this would be the sweat lodge and sweet grass that was traditionally practiced only among the Plains Indian tribes. Now it is influencing the native tribes of Northern Alberta, British Columbia, the Northwest Territories and the Yukon. Historically the sweat lodge and sweet grass had not been a part of their religious practice, but now because it is "Native", it is accepted and encouraged as part of their "Native" cultural experience.

The real issue at hand is a problem of identity. Although we have accepted Christ, many of us as native people still want to hang on to the traditions and the sacred elements within our culture. We are too proud to let go, because in them we have found a place of identity. Today we say, "*You have stolen my land, you have taken my language, but you cannot take away my culture (relating to spirituality)*". Many of our cultural (religious) traditions are being revived. If we place our whole identity on these traditions (and many do), then giving up our sacred elements and traditions becomes synonymous with giving up our identity because that is all we think we have left. Our spirituality is expressed in cultural ways.

The questions I ask Christian Native people are: "*Is it right to hang on to our sacred elements, ancient spiritual practices and traditions in order to maintain our sense of identity because of the wrong done to us in the past? Can we do this and also serve Christ? What about God's Word and God's ways? What about what Christ did for us on the Cross? Is His Blood good enough or not? Does God need these extra cultural things to help our people find healing as a people? When Christ died, did He die for the cause of redeeming our culture or for the cause of redeeming mankind from sin and death? Is not our clinging to culture the very thing that separates us from having a true relationship with Him?*"

II) *A CLOSER LOOK AT SYNCRETISM*

A common question I am asked is this: *is there not any aspect of a culture that could give glory to God? Could we not reclaim what Satan has stolen from us and use our culture to honor and worship of Jesus; i.e., CAN CULTURE BE REDEEMED?* The answer according to God's word is, NO. As people, we must know what our values are. If we don't know what are values are, we do not know what to pursue and we end up going along with anything and everything that comes our way. This is passiveness. I heard a friend once preach, *"Faith is your conviction, and it is <u>what</u> you believe."* The Bible talks of those who are tossed to and fro, carried about by every wind of doctrine (see Ephesians 4:14). They are wayward in the faith, not sure what it is that they really believe. This happens because they have not made Christ their foundation. Therefore, they will believe anything that looks good to them. Since Christ is the Word, our foundation should be in Him and should be based upon His Word. If there is no foundation, then it is hard to know the truth. We fall short because we rely on our own understanding. Proverbs 3:5 states, *"...lean not unto thine own understanding."* Leaning on our own understanding will lead to confusion and will allow syncretism (mixing) to become part of our values and beliefs because we will begin to put our faith in the *forms* of worship, rather than in God and in what He teaches in His Word.

What then is syncretism? This is defined as a blending of two religions: basically Christianity and another type of religion[42]. One author shares:

"Syncretism is the blending of two or more irreconcilable systems of belief and practice; the incompatible mixture of biblical truth with unbiblical practices"[43]

This *mixing* begins with *deception* and *compromise*. These are tools Satan uses to entangle people in bondage. He knows that once a person becomes born again, the power of the Holy Spirit is within them, and is leading them into the ways of God. Therefore, he tries to deceive people into believing it is acceptable to hold on to the old ways, the traditional ceremonies, dance, etc. He leads people into bondage using these various traditional forms of worship that are used to worship false gods. It is any wonder that interest is being revived in idol worship on many of our reserves today?

The word *deceive* means to: *mislead or delude*[44]. Satan knows that compromise stunts spiritual growth. Therefore, we must be careful and stay in the Word and in prayer to have the discernment needed to know what God honors. It is the Holy Spirit who teaches us to know the difference between the holy and the profane; therefore, we must stay in relationship with Him at all times.

I believe that syncretism is a devilish doctrine that is sweeping the body of Christ today. It is fair to say that syncretism uses the "sensational and the spectacular" elements of traditional native religion and blends them with Christian practices to produce a supernatural experience. (Satan uses the same tactics. He started with Adam and Eve in the garden. It looked pretty spectacular to see a serpent talking to them and his words were sensational.) The justification for syncretism is the belief that God is redeeming cultures to Himself. It is also justified by quoting Scripture passages completely out of context. Having been one that once radically believed in redemption of Native culture, I can surely give some examples of this type of deception.

First, let us examine the elements of traditional Native religion blended with Christian practices. Let's look at the traditional sacred drum (spirit drum as most non-Christian Natives call it). Non-Christian native tradition teaches that the native drum is in sync with "Mother Earth's" heart beat. One medicine man (Native witch doctor/spiritual healer/shaman) shares that the traditional drum was his Bible and helped him to foretell the future. The drum is often used in ceremonies, rituals, and dances. Within these, the drum is commonly used to stir up chanting and to invoke the power to summon spirits of the dead and spirits of animals, to search the future, to receive false prophecies, and to seek visions, etc. It is also used in ritual initiations to drown out the cries of those going through torturous procedures. It was never created to simply be a musical instrument, but for traditional ceremonial purposes. It has been said that the reason there are musical drum sets (ones you see with musical bands) is because the inventors of musical instruments found that the traditional sacred drum was not able to produce a musical sound that would compliment the remaining instruments, thus necessitating the invention of the musical drums. The purpose for them was to accommodate the rest of the musical band.

On the syncretism side, the traditional sacred drum is used for worship of the Creator God and Jesus Christ, His Son. It is believed that you can anoint it with oil and break the curse off this object and redeem it for spiritual warfare in the Kingdom of God. Another practice is to make a whole new traditional sacred drum that has never been used in ungodly practices. This sounds good in the soul realm; but, in the realm of the spirit, the traditional Native drum is a familiar object to the demon world. A friend of mine gave this example as she was responding to the question of redeeming the drum, "You take a moose caller (a tool hunters use to call moose) and decide to dedicate it (set it apart) for calling ducks and pray over it to call ducks; but, when you go hunting and blow that "redeemed" moose caller you are still going to attract moose, not ducks". So it is with the native traditional drum. Another friend gave this example: "Can a former gypsy fortune teller decide one day to redeem her crystal ball (or dedicate a new one) for Jesus, to anoint it with oil and break the curse off of it, and be led by the Spirit of God to use it for prophecies and visions; after all, its part of her cultural heritage?" That is ludicrous! Redeeming a crystal ball is impossible because it is an ungodly item never intended for godly purposes. I do not see any difference with our Native traditional drum or other cultural religious articles. In fact, according to the medicine men, the Native traditional drum is sacred and its use and purpose for existence is similar to that of the crystal ball.

Often syncretism is justified by quotation of Scripture passages out of context. "...*filleth all in all*..." This phrase is found in Ephesians 1:23 "*which is his body, the fullness of him that filleth all in all*". Those who believe in redeeming culture interpret this passage to mean that the Spirit of Christ fills all things in our cultures and is incorporated in the body of Christ. This misconception is taken from the very words, "*all in all*". What does this scripture mean by "*all in all*"? It is biased thinking to say that the words, "*all in all*" include Native traditional culture with all its components, and therefore each item can be redeemed for Christian worship. If one was to clearly understand Ephesians 1:23, the context of the words "*all in all*" is not referring to the sacred elements of any culture. Rather this passage is giving light to spiritual things pertaining to spiritual gifts given by the grace of God for the body of Christ - that Christ is the Head and we are His body. Romans 12 and I Corinthians 12 give clear insight concerning spiritual gifts that are void of any dependence upon the sacred elements of traditional culture within native religion or any other culture.

Having said all that... Syncretism is the tolerance and the blending of other religious cultural traditions with Christian practices and doctrines. Traditional spiritual practices and beliefs are a large part of native religion and culture. For example: the spirit of the buffalo and the spirit of the eagle, are common icons among most native communities, and are some of the many gods which are worshiped within native religion. Traditionalist's use these as spirit guides for power, wisdom, and strength. There are many other spirit guides and the list is very long, but I will mention only these two for the sake of time. We are now seeing some of these practices, beliefs and doctrines (heresies) coming into the Church through the tolerance and acceptance of regalia, sacred dances, and spirituals rituals, such as sweet grass smudging, and the use of the native spirit drum in Christian worship. In one particular Christian conference a special performance was put on by certain individuals involved with syncretism. As the people saw the performance, they were fascinated by what they saw and had little realization of the implications of what was actually happening on the stage. During the performance, the individuals on stage had called on the spirit of the eagle while burning sage (sage is a sacred herb, also defined as a sacred incense, which is used in smudging ceremonies in Native religion). They also began to call on the buffalo spirit to come over the people as the traditional Native spirit drum was beating. This was justified as being the performance of a "prophetic act" to release upon the people the attributes of the eagle and the buffalo. Basically, what they were doing was exactly what a medicine man does in his sacred lodge during a ritual. This was allowed in at this conference because this type of Native ritual is being "redeemed for Christ." Hello! Would the church allow a Buddhist ritual to be performed in their services? I think not. So why doesn't the church see native religion the same way?

> *"But though we, or an angel from heaven, preach any other gospel unto you than that which we have preached unto you, let him be accursed. As we said before, so say I now again, If any man preach any other gospel unto you than that ye have received, let him be accursed."* (Galatians 1:8-9).

The doctrine of syncretism is "another gospel" that is being preached to native people and in the churches. The rationale for it is to build a gospel bridge to native people, but instead it has become a stumbling block. I know of non-Christian Native traditionalists, who are turned off Christianity because of syncretism. They feel it is not true to their culture. They would rather their religion be "pure" traditional native religion, not a mish mash of ideas. Unfortunately there are those within the native culture who are considered semi-traditionalists and upon hearing this gospel of syncretism, they simply add Jesus as one of their other gods. After being told that God is redeeming cultures to Himself, they interpret that to mean it is acceptable to worship and to pray to Jesus through the use of sacred herbs, sacred songs (which are given by other spirits from the dark side), the sacred drum and dances (given to worship other spirits from the dark side) and to go inside sweat lodges to be purified and cleansed.

Syncretism is a tool the enemy uses to weaken the power of the true gospel message. Syncretism is acceptable because it does not offend the flesh. In fact, it often makes the flesh feel good for being so understanding and accepting compared to those "narrow minded" Christians who think Jesus is enough. Syncretism is inclusive and compromises with other ideas and doctrines. It avoids confrontations. Paul, in his writings to the Corinthian church, has stated that the cross of Christ will always bear a reproach. It will always confront and offend that which is ungodly in every aspect of our lives, both culturally and individually.

> *"For Christ sent me not to baptize, but to preach the gospel: not with wisdom of words, lest the cross of Christ should be made of none effect. For the preaching of the cross is to them that perish foolishness; but unto us which are saved it is the power of God...For the Jews require a sign, and the Greeks seek after wisdom: But we preach Christ crucified, unto the Jews a stumbling block, and unto the Greeks foolishness; But unto them which are called, both Jews and Greeks, Christ the power of God, and the wisdom of God"* (I Corinthians 1:17-18, 22-24).

A well-known non-Christian traditional Native-drummer/singer in the north approached a pastor one day and asked, "*Can Christians mix?*" (Meaning, can we combine the use of our sacred cultural elements with Christianity?) The pastor responded, "*What do you think?*" The man laughed and replied "*If they do, they'll never stand!*" If this man, who is not a Christian at all, realizes this important principle, what then is the matter with the Church? Only Jesus has the power to change our lives and to cause us to stand!

The Christianity we are called to walk in is a Christianity that lifts up Jesus and Him alone! In fact, according to Webster's Dictionary[45], Christianity means "the religion founded on the teachings of Jesus Christ". To really be a Christian is to follow and to obey Christ, nothing more or less. Sometimes just doing that goes against the fads and flows of the world. I believe the reason that syncretism has entered our churches so easily is due to the fact that it is popular in the world today to celebrate our diversity of cultures rather than the Lord who created all people. It has become a part of our accepted social and political policies. Today when Natives speak up for their rights, they are given full attention. So when Natives say, "*allow me to celebrate my culture in your church, you owe it to me and my people*" the Church listens. The Church is eager to embrace the Native culture, not only because it is popular policy, but also to make amends for their guilt over past injustices done to the Native people. Some feel that allowing the expression of Native culture in the church will bring revival to the Native people and will turn them to God. Certainly this method seems for some to be easier or more popular than God's method as given in II Chronicles 7 verse 14: *"If My people who are called by My name put away their pride and pray, and look for My face, and turn from their sinful ways, then I will hear from heaven. I will forgive their sin, and will heal their land."*[46] However, God's ways will work whereas man's ways will fail. Many in the church are now convinced that the only way our Native people can be healed is by making room for native culture in Christianity. Do we not realize that Christ paid the price of our HEALING and our REDEMPTION so *people* will be healed and saved from eternal death without God? Have we forgotten the message of the Gospel in its *fullest* capacity?

Today, we hear it said that it is acceptable to hold on to pagan sacred elements and to still take our stand as Christ-centered Christians who embrace Christianity. It was not always this way. In Acts 19:13-16 we read of an incident which occurred between the seven sons of Sceva and a demoniac. They were trying to practice Christianity in the context of their culture, without making the heart and life change that true Christianity brings about (See II Corinthians 5:17). They were trying to cast out evil spirits, which is part of what true followers of Jesus are called to do (See Mark 16:17). They were unable to do this and, in fact, were overpowered by these evil spirits. Several things happened. First of all this caused great fear, not only to the seven sons of Sceva, but also to the many others who witnessed or heard about the incident. Acts 19:17 speaks of this fear. The word *fear* from Acts 19:17 taken from the

Strong's Concordance; Greek word # 5401 *phobos*
– "to be put in fear; alarm or fright"[47]. This great
fear prompted by the incident they had witnessed
brought on a respect and a reverence of the supernatural. Their eyes were opened to the reality of the
spiritual darkness they were living in and were practicing. This fear (phobos) brought on a revival! Many
began discarding their occult books and renounced
their practice of mysterious arts. The people began to
confess their wicked deeds. The value of all that was
burned amounted to fifty thousand pieces of silver.
The Word of God grew mightily within the region
of Ephesus. This revival was so wide-spread that the
craftsmen, who made shrines to the goddess Diana,
began to go bankrupt; therefore, Demetrius caused a
great stir in the city and rallied an outbreak against
the Christians and their leaders. Although they tried
to cause a commotion, the town-clerk could not
find any reason to justify their actions against the
Christians. Whenever and wherever the apostles went
about to preach the gospel, they proclaimed that all
men should *repent*.

Scripturally, repentance involves a change of
mind, heart and behavior which can be seen in Acts
19 and many other scriptures as well, i.e.: Acts 2:28-
42, 44-47 and Mark 1:15-20, etc. It is time for us,
as the Church of the Living God, to wake up and to
realize that *we* must walk in true repentance if the
Gospel of Jesus Christ is to be preached and to be
lived in power as the scriptures have proclaimed it
to be.

The message on my heart for the church and for my Native people (Native Christians in particular) relates to the message given to the Laodicean Church (see Revelations 3:14-22). In these scriptures, they were a lukewarm church. The Lord Jesus' response to their lukewarmness can be seen when He said to them, "*I know thy works, that thou are neither cold nor hot: I would thou wert cold or hot. So then because thou art lukewarm, and neither cold or hot, I will spew thee out of my mouth.*" (Revelations 3:15-16). Compromise results in a lukewarm gospel. The gospel message is to remain **pure**. Nothing is to be added or to be taken away. The message of the gospel focuses entirely on the death, burial and resurrection of Jesus. Jesus did not die to redeem our cultural traditions, or our sacred cultural elements. He died, rather, to redeem the individual person from their sin and all its bondages. Often it is our culture that keeps us from having a true relationship with our Heavenly Father. Our lives are to be conducted according to His ways; if that means making some changes, then so be it. There is a curse that comes on people when they preach or teach another gospel (see Galatians 1:8 and Revelations 22:18, 19). If we add or take away from God's word there is severe judgment. This is exactly what syncretism is: it is "another gospel" that is being taught and is being preached everywhere and it is bringing confusion to many, both inside and outside the Body of Christ. It is adding that which is not of God to the true gospel message. It is time to look at ourselves and at God's Word and to see *what* He has come to redeem, to heal and to restore.

He has come to redeem and to heal us as individuals (see Isaiah 53). He will also heal our land as we humble ourselves, repent and turn from our wicked ways (see II Chronicles 7:14). He came to restore our relationship with Him and to establish our identity *in* Christ (see Galatians 2:20). I no longer say that I am Native, but rather I say, I am a Christian Native. My identity lies in the fact that Jesus redeemed me from the bonds of sin and death, and brought me out of the kingdom of darkness and into the Kingdom of His marvelous light. I am born again; I am a child of the most High God! His Kingdom culture has become my culture (see Colossians 3:11) and (see Galatians 3:28).

No longer am I subject to the ordinances, the rituals, the sacraments, the traditions of my culture; nor do I bow to other gods. I am a servant of the Living God, and I follow His ways and live for Him. *"For in Him we live, and move, and have our being;..."* Acts 17:28

III) *IDOLATRY OF THE HEART*

Syncretism is idolatry in our hearts. We cling to what we have created – our culture and we bow to it in our hearts. This is especially true for Native people who are struggling to find their identity in their culture.

Anything that stands between God and us is idolatry. Nothing or no one should ever take the place of Jesus in our lives. We must let go of our old cultural identity and move on in our Christian walk. II Peter

3:18 states that we are to "grow in the grace and in the knowledge of our Lord, Jesus Christ". Of Who? Jesus. Not the ways of man. Everything by which we are to live and conduct our lives is through Jesus Christ. We grow in God's grace, not in the grace of our culture and tradition. We grow in the knowledge of Jesus Christ, not in the knowledge of cultural tradition. No matter how beautiful or close to Biblical principles, our culture will not set us free from sin nor will it heal any of our wounds (see Acts 4:12). Our own cultures could never measure up to what we gain in Christ Jesus. I heard a Christian Native elder say, "*Maaaah! We just need Jesus!*" Christ should be the ultimate center of our hearts. Let us face the truth. We know that syncretism is wrong; deep down we know it is not approved in God's Word. Holding on to our old native religion through keeping its significant sacraments, religious traditions and dances does not give glory to God in any way, shape or form. *We cannot worship God in spirit and in truth if we hold idolatry in our hearts.*

God is a jealous God and He wants our total affection given to Him. We are to love Him with all our hearts, souls, and minds in order to truly worship Him *in spirit and in truth*. Without God first place in our hearts and lives, it is impossible to experience the true worship of our Heavenly Father that Jesus described in John 4:23-24. We can have a form of worship; we can enjoy our worship; but, we will not be able to worship Him in spirit and in truth. We cannot give affection towards our culture which hinders us from a pure relationship with God. God is above culture, so we should lay aside the emphasis of our culture when we worship Him in order to maintain a pure relationship with Him. ***The key to abstaining from idolatry in our hearts is to love <u>Him</u> with <u>all</u> our heart, mind, and soul and spirit.***

Hebrews 12:2 exhorts us to LOOK unto Jesus who is the author and finisher of our faith. We are not to look anywhere else to increase our worship experience towards God. Simply *looking unto Jesus* will do just that. Psalm 145:10-11 states, "*All thy works shall praise thee, O Lord; and thy saints shall bless thee. They shall speak of the glory of thy kingdom, and talk of thy power;*" What God does in and through us will bring praise and glory to Himself and will not to bring any praise and glory to our flesh. What God alone does through us will speak of the glory of <u>His</u> Kingdom, not the glory of our cultures. What God alone can do through us will talk of <u>His</u> Power, not the power of our humanity. This will happen as long as we are yielded to Him. Absolutely no attention should be drawn to us so that no part of our culture, or our individuality will receive any glory or praise. **We must be hidden behind the cross.** We do not want people to see us; we want them to see Jesus! God will always glorify Himself and honor His own name through His creation. The trouble is that we try to attribute honor to everything else but to God. Often we end up glorifying creation (God's or our own) rather than God, the true Creator. Although we make an effort to say "*we give God the glory*", He is still not glorified. Our intentions may be that God would move in and through us as His people and that he would approve and bless our efforts done in His Name, but inwardly we still often want people to recognize the glory of our culture, the beauty of our regalia and dances, the power of our drum and our Native ways; in this, self is still exalted. This is the sin of Lucifer. Isaiah 14 tells of his attempt to exalt himself above God because of his own pride. We see further in Ezekiel 28 how God dealt with him for trying to claim the power and the glory that belonged to God alone. Lucifer idolized himself. Is this not the same root of idolatry that causes us to strive to keep our own identity, rather than taking upon us our new identity through Christ? (See I Corinthians 1:14-17). God help us all. *We must become more Christ-centered rather than self-centered!*

IV) *WHERE STRONGHOLDS REMAIN*

> "(*For the weapons of our warfare are not carnal, but mighty through God to the pulling down of strongholds;) Casting down imaginations, and every high thing that exalteth itself in the knowledge of God, and bringing into captivity every thought to the obedience of Christ;*" (II Corinthians 10:4, 5).

Oftentimes we wonder why our "warfare" to see our native people reached and to see their lives and respective communities transformed by the Gospel of Christ, is not more successful. I believe that one of the reasons is syncretism. We cannot take carnal things from our culture and attempt to redeem them back for the glory of God; nor can we take them and try to accomplish by them those things that only the Spirit of God can do. Romans chapter 8 reminds us that our carnality and fleshly things are to "die" so that the Spirit can live in and through us. This is especially true if we are still relying on objects of affection, such as the use of the spirit drum (which was originally crafted for use in initiations, spiritual ceremonies and witchcraft rituals), in worship. Natives call witchcraft "bad medicine" or "curses" and these practices will never draw people to God.

Let's look at one of the battles of the children of Israel in Ai (Joshua 7) with Joshua as their leader. In Joshua chapter 6 they had just taken Jericho. A great victory was won with the help of the Lord! In Joshua 6:18 the Lord gave them specific instructions to take the spoil of the battle: they were to keep themselves from the accursed thing; if they took anything deemed accursed, they would make themselves accursed and cause trouble in Israel. Their next battle was to take Ai. Joshua 7:1-26, we read starting in verse one how Achan, from the tribe of Judah, "...*committed a trespass in the accursed thing:... and the anger of the Lord was kindled against the children of Israel*". Ai, in this passage of Scripture, according to Vines Dictionary # 5857, means: *a heap of ruins; do amiss, bow down, make crooked, commit iniquity, pervert,*.[48] This is the city they were about to go against and the Lord gave the instruction that they were to take no accursed thing. According to Strongs Concordance Hebrew word #2764, *the accursed thing* was usually a *doomed object.*[49] Because of Achan's sin, Israel lost this battle big time! Joshua sought the Lord as to why they lost (Vs. 11). Smart man! The Lord revealed to Joshua that there was an accursed thing taken and put among their stuff. He clarified to Joshua that He would not be with them any more unless they *destroyed* the accursed thing from among them (Vs. 12). Therefore the children of Israel could not stand before their enemies in Ai, because they were accursed. What was the heart of the matter for Achan? Vs. 21 states that when he *saw* a Babylonish *garment* and two hundred shekels of silver and a wedge of gold of fifty shekels he *coveted* them and took them and then hid these items in the ground inside his tent. The heart of idolatry is to covet. Covet simply means to desire something that you cannot have. Achan's sin cost a lot of lives and caused Israel to loose a battle. They were utterly humiliated and defeated before their enemy. The Babylonish garment is similar to many elements within culture and with the silver and gold comes power. If we are coveting these things and do not deal with the sin of the heart, then we are setting ourselves up for destruction before we even realize it. Let's learn from this example in scripture. Think not that we are exempt. Joshua dealt with the problem and eradicated it. In the following chapter they went out against Ai again and this time they won!

In terms of what is happening today regarding items used in Native religion being incorporated into the practice of Christianity, we find that the fetishes people are trying to redeem were used for demonic purposes: seeking animal spirits, communicating with dead ancestors, seeking visions, seeking quests, and participating in ceremonial rituals. These same fetishes are being used in feasts, celebrations and pow-wows, hung on walls and inside vehicles for protection against evil. They are also being used for decorations, and/or for story telling. These fetishes are familiar objects in the spirit realm and give an open door for demonic oppression in one's life and home because they are cursed objects. The only way to deal with cursed objects is to get rid of them. One Christian Native elder, who was a former hereditary chief, shared how the shaman (medicine man) of old would receive visions from the supernatural world and a spirit animal would appear, giving guidance to show him what to carve on wood or stone for a family clan. It is believed that "spirit power" is embedded within these carvings. Ivan Doxtator gives this following insight:

"There is a demonic aspect to the culture where the spirit becomes associated with a physical material and gives an energy factor by Satan to keep the group in bondage. The point is that there are things that our ancestors have been involved in that they can develop emotional and spiritual soul ties to a drum or some type of instrument. Because that instrument is committed to a particular spirit of deity, there is more there than just giving it up. These same spirits which are related to it can come back into play and be involved in that thing"[50]

A common statement is often made; "*You can anoint it with oil and plead the blood of Jesus and the curse is broke*", but is that really true? I once believed and practiced this heresy. Can it be so and how does God's Word condone such a teaching? God's Word, in fact, does not condone that teaching. As a matter of fact, after diligent research, I have come to find it states the opposite. The previous account of Joshua's battle in Ai is one example. I have also made many attempts to find scripture passages in the Word of God to agree with the practice of syncretism and was unsuccessful. In fact, the more I searched in the Word of God, the more it became clear that *I* was deceived. It is amazing what searching the scriptures with a sincere heart does to you. Thank God that He sent us the Spirit of Truth to guide us into all truth (see John 14:26; 6:13; 8:31-31). Jesus came to set us free from the things that hold us in bondage.

Nowhere in scripture will you find that we can redeem an ungodly object of worship by breaking the curse off it and personally use it for the glory of God. It is heresy to teach from scripture that accursed things are redeemable. The Bible is very clear about these things. What is redeemable according to scripture is *people*. He came to set us free from the curse of the law of sin and death. Curses are broken off people, not objects of ungodly worship. Cursed objects were burnt until they were totally consumed (see again, Joshua 7:1-26). One author gives this insight:

> "*Some fetishes are considered primitive art and may be of considerable monetary value.*

While they are believed by some to possess magical powers, to others they are simply decorative pieces. They may be natural things like stones, shells, feathers, or animal claws, or they may be wood, stone, or metal carvings. But to the people who made them, they represent their gods and possess supernatural powers. These items do have power, not in themselves, but they are the dwelling places of demons and serve to transfer demonic power from one person to another."[51]

Common sense in spiritual warfare is to make sure your life is clean of anything that will open a door to Satan. One of the ways of closing the door is to get rid of any sacrament, any fetish, or any religious objects that have been used to worship or have been used to honor another god. You cannot use these things for the glory of God because they were originally used (dedicated) to the worship of false gods. They are cursed.

In I Samuel 15, Saul was sent by God to battle the Amalekites with clear instructions from the Lord. Those instructions were that they were not to spare anything, not the women and children, or even their livestock. They were to utterly destroy all that the Amalakites had. Why? The Amalakites fought against the Hebrews when they were in the wilderness in a time of distress after the exodus from Egypt.[52] Saul and his army went in and took the Amalakites by force, destroyed the whole city and burnt almost everything. However, not all was destroyed as commanded by God. Saul spared the King of Amalek and the livestock. He did not fully obey the Word of the Lord, but did what was right in his own eyes. Samuel, the prophet of that day was furious with Saul for doing so, and the word of the Lord came to him to tell Saul that his rebellion was as the sin of witchcraft, and his stubbornness as the sin of idolatry in the eyes of God (see I Samuel 15:23). Because of Saul's disobedience, God took his kingship from him and sent the prophet Samuel to anoint another king for the nation of Israel.

This was serious. Saul went to war, spared a few things of the Amalekites and because of this he lost his crown. His crown represented his authority. Revelation 1:6 says that we are now made kings and priests unto our God. What makes us think that we can spare a few fetishes and sacred ornaments used to worship other gods when God would not even allow the livestock of the Amalekites to be spared? No wonder many struggle to walk in true God-given authority today!

Spiritual warfare is won by humility; it cannot be won with compromise. Like Saul, we, too, will lose the spiritual authority that we have gained in Christ, if we cling to what He abhors. You can close the front door of your house against the robbers and thieves, but, if you leave the back door open, they can still get in and wreak havoc in your life. There are many testimonies from people who have struggled with sickness as a result of keeping occult objects, religious statues, and special kinds of jewelry, spiritual paintings, etc. that were not of God in their homes.

Once they rid themselves of those things, they were healed, and the demonic oppression lifted.

How simple it is. These things cannot be redeemed for the glory of God, no matter how spiritual people think they are, and no matter how people may try to justify them with scripture.

There was a time in my own life when a dear friend of mine had given me a beautiful necklace. As I was at a house fellowship one night, I had incredible arthritic pain in my hands, wrists, arms, elbows, knees and legs. I had been suffering from this pain from a young age. That night I finally had enough of this torment and requested prayer to be healed. I had experienced a touch from the Lord a couple years prior to this, but for some reason, the pain of arthritis was back and it seemed to be worse. I was new to the group of people I was with. As they began to pray, the leader of this group had a vision of a piece of jewelry that fit the exact description of my necklace, though I was not wearing it that evening. The leader advised that the jewelry I had was probably the cause of my illness and that I should get rid of it. The Holy Spirit revealed that there was a curse upon the necklace. The very next day I went to my jewelry case and smashed the necklace to pieces, *even though it held sentimental value*. It was then that I was released from the pain I suffered. I realized then that it was not worth the suffering.

Earlier in the section on Strongholds, we read II Corinthians 10:5 which show that another aspect of strongholds is that they are in the mind; they are imaginations; they are high things that are exalted against the knowledge of God.

As I have stated earlier, faith includes our convictions; it is what we believe. If we really believe God's Word, then we are to live according to God's Word. His Word is His standard for our daily lives and it will confront and change our way of thinking. Anything in our thought life, in our beliefs and behavior that is not in accordance with the ways of God is in need of change. The strongholds that exalt themselves against God have to go. These are often buried in our cultural mindsets. When dealing with cultural mindsets in light of religion we realize that there is a lot of faith put in methods, beliefs, sacraments, indicators and initiators. (We will review more about indicators and initiators below.) *Spiritual significance* is attached to each fetish and to each ritual. When you understand this significance then you can see where the stronghold is hidden or not hidden. The following two examples illustrate this: The people of the North have what is called an inukshuk. Originally, the inukshuk was used in the vast Arctic tundra as a marker on the land to indicate that man had been there before. It often showed where water could be found, or where caribou could be sighted for hunting. It helped the Inuit people find their way around as their natural habitat had no trees for landmarks. Its significance was natural, not spiritual. Today, you will find replicas of them on the market with a spiritual writing attached to it for the sake of making it more enticing to buyers (namely tourists) who buys them as exotic pieces of art. Any spiritual significance has been attached to it to increase sales, not for any spiritual purposes.

A second example, *sweet grass*, provides an example of a natural object which has great spiritual significance. This grass is used as a sacrament in Native Religion. This *sacrament* consists of burning braided sweet grass, which gives off a vanilla smell and is quite similar to incense. It is considered a holy herb among the native peoples. The *belief* is that sweet grass will bless one's home, protect one from evil spirits or bad luck and will cleanse an area or person from evil spirits or sickness. The *method* is to smudge the smoke that rises from the sweet grass over one's body and around the building one is in. Sweet grass is an *indicator* that there is direct communication to the spirit world where prayers are offered while the smoke rises in the air. Those that follow Native Religion often *initiate* this practice. In actuality, instead of being protected from evil spirits one is actually opening up one's home and life to these evil spirits. The stronghold lies in the faith one puts in the power of sweet grass to protect and to cleanse and the spirit which often attaches itself to it. Today, this is also sold in the market places; only in this case, the write-up regarding its spiritual significance is true.

Usually, when bad things occur in one's life, the blame is attributed to the possibility that one has been cursed. (Natives call curses *bad medicine*). In reality, the influence of evil spirits may have been allowed into one's life by misplaced faith in sacraments like sweet grass. God's Word shows us that we have the covering of the blood of Jesus; He is the Great Shepherd who watches over our lives (see Psalm 23, Psalm 91, Isaiah 54:17, Revelations 12:11). All we need is faith in Christ alone, to accept what He did on the cross and to resist those evil spirits in the Name of Jesus. James 4:7, 8 states, *"Submit yourselves therefore unto God. Resist the devil, and he will flee from you. Draw nigh unto God, and he will draw nigh unto you. Cleanse your hands, ye sinners; and purify your hearts, ye double minded."* To be double minded is to be unsure about who you are, what you believe and deludes your ability to discern properly what is not of God. This is especially true concerning items that are dear to us.

Another example of how the use of fetishes can cause problems in one's life is the use of dream catchers. Dream catchers are very popular as pieces of art and often used in the home. In Native religion, it is believed that the bead(s) in the middle of the circle inside the webbed material are the eye(s) of a spirit guide(s) to watch over you and to catch all your bad dreams at night. Obviously, in Native culture a dream catcher is far more than a piece of art - it is a spirit house for a spirit guide which is "welcome" and it is an object of spiritual significance and power. The incredible thing is that Christians take these objects into their homes believing they are harmless decorations. As stated earlier, these are familiar objects to the spirit world and give access for evil spirits to enter your home, even Christian homes.

Another example of the harm caused by the use of fetishes is the spirit drum. In the light of strongholds we must understand its spiritual significance. How quick and easy it is to believe there is nothing wrong with spirit drums. The spiritual significance of the spirit drum in Native culture is that it is believed that the drum's beat is in sync with "Mother Earth's" heart. It is used in séances, pow-wows, round dances, rituals, ceremonies and other rituals. It is also believed that the use of the spirit drum in Native religion can summon spirits and one is able to communicate with those spirits. Also, the loud drum beat will drown out the cries of pain inflicted on initiates by evil spirits. Let's look at it in more detail.

As has been said, the spirit drum (or sacred drum) to the native people is significant because of the belief that as it is used the spirits will come. This is the purpose of the sacred drum. The method is to beat it in rhythm with the heart beat; it is an *indicator* to all who practice Native Religion, that there is, through the drum, direct communication with the spirit world. Those who practice Native Religion have *initiated* this communication with the spirit world for centuries. The sacred drum enables them to "get in the spirit" to have direct contact with the supernatural. Often sacred songs come forth from the spirit world as one makes this connection through the sacred drum. For the medicine man or for past or present followers of Native Religion, the use of the drum is an *indication* of this direct communication with the spirit world, as is the use of sweet grass, rattles and regalia. This is precisely why it is an important issue for the church to understand. Do we really want to promote, to defend and to use such powerful *indica-*

tors of the worship of other gods to draw people to Christ? Would it not be better to fast and to pray and to seek God's face according to II Chronicles 7:14? It may not seem as exciting a process, but the results would are definitely more beneficial. Let us continue look at some of those issues.

The drum and the dance are combined with each other. Dances usually imitate the movements of one's totem animal; for example, the Crow Hop. I attended pow-wows and round dances in my adolescent years and as I watched the dancers begin to move and to sway to the chanting pow-wow singers and to the beat of the spirit drum, more than 80% would go into a trance, their movements controlled by the false spirits possessing them. This is fascinating to the eye and is considered by the captive audience as "being in the spirit". I remember the pride and the spiritual high I would get as I watched the proud dancers move around the inner circle. For others, it starts as a sport, but eventually, they come under the influence of the drum's power.

Regalia are always worn in every dance. Regalia are ceremonial clothing and have spiritual significance, as well. The type of spiritual dance to be performed dictates color codes, patterns and styles. If any of the dancers have a feather fall from their outfit they must perform a small ceremonial dance around the feather before they continue their competitive performance with the other dancers. To have had a feather drop from your outfit is considered a very serious thing. The fear of consequences for dropping a feather is not just from the judges who watch the competitive sport but also from the supernatural forces. In fact, some dancers have been mysteriously injured as they have tried to deal with this type of mishap. This is the norm of Native cultural tradition and religion.

It is important to understand that regalia are not the everyday clothing of the Native people. Native people wear clothing the same as the rest of the country. To wear regalia is to identify with ceremonial customs. The first person I met from Germany had come to Canada on a missionary outreach to minister to Native children and I was the first Native she met. At the Bible camp she expected to see little brown skinned children wearing tanned hides with markings on their faces. Instead, she saw them wearing normal clothing like every one else. She was amazed at this discovery.

People often misinterpret Hudson Taylor's method of identifying with the Chinese people. It is true that he dressed just like them and grew his hair long. He wore what was their everyday clothing, but it is never indicated that he wore the ceremonial clothing worn in the Buddhist temples. There are non-Native people who wear regalia trying to identify with native people. By doing this they do not realize that they are actually identifying with the Native religion. Often, because of ignorance, we desire or allow those things that are not glorifying to God in our Christian services. When we use spiritually significant objects which were used to worship other gods and are known indicators to those who are culturally familiar with the things that communicate with other spirits, we are inadvertently preaching another gospel. How sad to believe it is necessary to have these items included in our Christian worship when they are demonically and religiously based!

Religious beliefs are also expressed in Native arts and crafts. There are some arts and crafts which have no spiritual significance at all. In fact at this moment, as I type this, I am wearing moccasins made by an Inuit lady from the Arctic. I have in my hair a beautiful barrette with a floral design, made with moose hair tufting and hide by the Dene` people. This is clothing and outerwear. Soon I'll be hanging on my wall a gorgeous work of art, a floral design made of porcupine quills and moose hair tufting on a piece of black velvet, that I received as a gift. *Yet, still many items do have a spiritual significance.* The key to identifying whether a piece of art or craftwork has any spiritual significance is to pin point the history of it: where did it come from, did it go through any ceremonies, what is depicted and what is the use of the craftwork? It is wise to check out all gifts, ornaments, fetishes, ceremonies and the like to avoid allowing evil spirits to work in your life.

God is a *Holy* God and He will in no way have any flesh or ungodly substances glory in His presence. Yes, He did say in His Word that He will pour out His Spirit upon all flesh (Joel 2:28), but that is speaking of *people* for whom He shed His blood and not man made objects which are intended for ungodly purposes or ceremonies which often carry demonic activity. It is written in His Word, "...*what communion hath light with darkness?*" (II Corinthians 6:14). **God is a Holy God and He desires that His people worship Him on the basis of His holiness**.

PART FIVE

MOVING FORWARD

"Wherefore seeing we also are compassed about with so great cloud of witnesses, let us lay aside every weight, and the sin which doth so easily beset us, and let us run with patience the race that is set before us, Looking unto Jesus the author and finisher of our faith; who for the joy that was set before him endured the cross, despising the shame, and is set down at the right hand of the throne of God" Hebrews 12:1, 2

I) *NO TURNING BACK*

There are precepts and values within Native culture that are not ungodly at all. For example, there are unwritten laws about honoring and respecting our elders and providing for their needs. Other unwritten laws that have been orally passed down include things like: "honor your father and mother; don't neglect the widows and orphan children; share what you have; help each other make life less difficult; equality among all people; listen while others are talking and do not interrupt; everyone has the right to be heard; be polite and don't argue; sleep at night and work during the day; when hunting, do not shoot female game with young; respect the cycle of the seasons and ways of the animals; maintain your keen sense of humor; take care of your body because the Creator made you; respect and honor your leaders and learn from their wisdom". These are values of a basically caring and giving people, which are basic moral principles to live by in order to make this world a better place to live in. There are many scriptural principles reflected in these values. They are also common values in many places in the world. Sad to say, it is sin that has brought corruption in values such as these. Only Christ came to redeem humanity from sin in order that we could maintain these values and live by them.

The Hebrew were given a set of regulations and patterns from God the Creator. These elements, traditions and ordinances were God-given through His servant Moses. As I read in Exodus about the instructions for the Tabernacle and all its components, I was amazed at every intricate detail that was to be precisely followed. I thought to myself: *"This is humanly impossible and then in the middle of this God also gives the Ten Commandments."* As I read I came across the verses stating that God Himself filled men with wisdom, understanding and skillful knowledge to make each element He designed for the Tabernacle (see Exodus 36). One would have had to be filled by God with these attributes in order to accurately follow each detail. Near the end of Exodus the tabernacle and all its vessels were anointed and were sanctified as holy; then Aaron and his sons were also anointed and were set apart to minister to the Lord in the Tabernacle. In the book of Leviticus, more regulations were given regarding sacrifices and offerings. It became clear to me that each element, tradition, ordinance, sacrificial rite and offering were according to a *God-given* pattern, including the garments for the office of the priests.

Now let's move forward in time from the days of Moses to Christ. The book of Hebrews clearly reveals that a new way of worship was established through the blood of Christ. Christ had come to fulfill the law and offer his own blood as the final sacrifice for sin, not only for the Jewish people, but also for the whole world. The New Life Bible writes it in this fashion:

> *"Christ makes this New Way of Worship sure for us because of God's promise. There had to be many religious leaders during the time of the Old Way of Worship. They died and others had to keep on in their work. But Jesus lives forever. He is the Religious Leader forever. It will never change. And so Jesus is able, now and forever, to save from the punishments of sin all who come to God through Him because He lives forever to pray for them. We need such a Religious Leader Who made the way for man to go to God.*

Jesus is Holy and has no guilt. He has never sinned and is different from sinful men. He has the place of honor above the heavens. Christ is not like other religious leaders. They had to give gifts every day on the altar in worship for their own sins first and then for the sins of the people. Christ did not have to do that. He gave one gift on the altar and that gift was Himself. It was done once and it was for all time. The Law makes religious leaders of men. These men are not perfect. After the law was given, God spoke with a promise. He made His Son a perfect Religious Leader forever." (Hebrews 7:22-28).[53]

"*But Christ came as the Head Religious Leader of the good things God promised. He made the way for man to go to God. He was a greater and more perfect tent. He was not made by human hands and was not a part of this earth. Christ went into the Holiest Place of All one time for all people. He did not take the blood of goats and young cows to give to God as a gift in worship. He gave His own blood. By doing this, He bought us with His own blood and made us free from sin forever. With the Old Way of Worship, the blood and ashes of animals could not make men clean after they had sinned. How much more the blood of Christ will do! He gave Himself as a perfect gift to God through the Spirit that lives forever. Now your heart can be free from the guilty feeling of doing work*

114

that is worth nothing. Now you can work for the Living God. Christ is the One Who gave us this New Way of Worship. All those who have been called by God may receive life that lasts forever just as He promised them. Christ bought us with His blood when He died for us. This made us free from our sins which we did under the Old Way of Worship" (Hebrew 9:11-15)[54]

The old way of worship and its ceremonies is done away with. Christ came to establish a new way for all who put their faith in Him. After reading these scriptures from Hebrews, it is clear why Jesus Himself had said "...*I am the way, the truth and the Life, no man cometh unto the Father butt by me*" (John 14:6).

II *WHAT ELSE DOES THE BIBLE HAVE TO SAY AND WHAT DOES CULTURE HAVE TO SAY?*

Jesus said, "...*ye are of this world; I am not of this world*" (John 8:23b). "*My Kingdom is not of this world: if my Kingdom was of this world, my servants would fight...*" (John 18:36a) What do we do with these words of Jesus? The word **world,** in both these scriptures share the same meaning. The Greek word *kosmos* is found in #**2889** of the Strong's Exhaustive Concordance[55] as: "orderly arrangement, i.e. decoration; by implication: the world (in a wide or narrow sense, including it's' inhabitants, literally or figura-

115

tively)" (Also translated as: "adorning, world"). In some contexts the world is simply the place where people live and in other contexts the world, with its way of doing things and its decorations, is a system seen to be opposed to God and His Kingdom purposes. These things are usually in harmony with a part of culture.

Jesus said (John 8:38 and John 18:36), that His Kingdom was not of the cultures of this world because they were opposed to it; His Kingdom was, in fact, separate and He had come to reveal His Kingdom to all mankind. The Kingdom of God is still separate from the cultures of this world; the world still is opposed to the Kingdom of God. His Kingdom-culture surpasses our own cultural mind-sets and ways of doing things. As stated, Jesus does not change to our way of life, but rather, we are the ones who are changed by the transforming power of His Spirit so we can live according to the ways of His Kingdom. Interesting that we find in John 18:36, Jesus also said, "...*if my Kingdom was of this world, my servants would fight*..." Often we try to fight for our rights; our right to express our individuality in whatever manner we are accustomed to. When it comes to matters of the Kingdom of God, instead of fighting for our rights, we simply lay them down at the foot of the cross; we take up His Kingdom purposes for our lives. The self-life, with all its interests, no longer determines our values and goals; instead our life becomes all about Jesus and His reflection in our daily living, as well as matters of worship.

In this section, we will begin to review certain words found in specific scriptures from God's Word such as: "elements" "traditions", "rudiments", and "ordinances" in order to clarify what they mean when relating to cultural activities within Native Religion.

The following verses are a confirmation that the old way of worship became obsolete because of the sacrifice of Christ's blood in our stead:

1) **ELEMENTS**: *"Even so we, when we were children, were in bondage under the elements of the world:"* (Galatians 4:3). We are no longer in bondage to the *elements* of this world. **This applies even to the elements of our culture**. Nelson's Three-in-One Bible Reference Companion defines this word as *"basic parts of anything"*[56]. The Greek word used is *"stoicheion"* #4747, in Strong's Exhaustive concordance[57]. This word from the Greek speaks of "something orderly in arrangements..." implying a basic "fundamentally initial constitute" and is also translated as "element, principle, rudiment". This definition can be taken to mean the *basic **parts** of anything* within our culture. There are many things that are *orderly in arrangements* within our culture. The word *"world"* in this scripture comes from the Greek word #2889 *"kosmos"*, and is the same Greek word as in John 18:36, *"My Kingdom is not of this **world**..."* From the Greek word # 2889, *"Kosmeo"* (2885) is also derived,[58] meaning: "to make beautiful, decorate, dress; trim (a lamp); (pass.) to put in order; be adorned,

decorated, beautifully dressed: - adorned". This has a lot to do with culture. This part of culture is also a part of Native religion as we especially consider the sacred drum, regalia, rattles, dream catchers, sacred dances and such. These cultural elements are specially designed and adorned but not according to the glory of Christ; they are of this world which is opposed to His Kingdom. The Amplified Bible gives Galatians 4:3 in this fashion: *"So we (Jewish Christians) also, when we were minors, were **kept like slaves** under [the rules of the Hebrew ritual and subject to] the elementary teachings of a system of **external observations** and **regulations**"* (emphasis added). Interesting how it is given that we were *"kept like slaves"* to these *"external observations and regulations"*. They keep us in bondage as long as we continue to practice these certain elements that are observed within our culture. These are of the world and keep us in bondage. The reason these elements hold us in bondage is because they cannot keep us free from sin, neither can they reconcile us to God. <u>Instead, they keep us from *the truth* that can set us free.</u>

2) **TRADITION**: Colossians 2:8 *"Beware lest any man spoil you through philosophy and vain deceit, after the **tradition** of men, after the rudiments of the world, **and not after Christ**"*(emphasis added). First of all the word *spoil* is in the Strongest Strong's Concordance, Greek word# 4812 *"svlagōgeō"* – "to be taken captive". [59] Strong's Exhaustive Concordance defines this

word: "to lead away as booty, i.e. (figuratively) to seduce"[60]; It is derived from the Greek word # 4813, "*svlaō*" – "to rob : robbed"[61]; it is also from the Greek word # 71, "*agō*"– "to bring, lead; as a command: look, pay attention, listen"[62]. In other words *spoil* means to: carry you off and rob you of the truth of the knowledge of Christ Jesus; drawing your attention away from Him, making you a captive of deception. Let's go further and look at the word **tradition**. Nelson's Three-in-One Bible Reference Companion defines this word as "*precept, or customs passed down from generations.*"[63] The Greek Word #3862 from Strong's Exhaustive Concordance is "*paradosis*" – "a precept; or an ordinance"[64]. Note that the "tradition of men" in this verse pertains to those traditions that are not revealed in the written Word of God. Even if a "tradition" has been observed by men for many generations, it does not necessarily make it acceptable to continue to practice it in the eyes of God. We are told in this scripture to "*Beware lest any man spoil you…after the tradition of men…*" Why then do we continue to practice the tradition of men? God has given us a new way of worship (see Hebrews 10:20).

3) **RUDIMENTS**: This word is also taken from Colossians 2:8 "…*the rudiments of the world*". Nelson's Three-in-One Bible Reference defines this word as "*principles*"[65]. The word *tradition*, as we have previously studied, is synonymous with the *rudiments* and is derived from the same Greek word # 3862[66]. Colossians 2:20, reveals

that we are *dead with Christ* from the traditions (rudiments) of the world; *this includes culture* because it is of the world and not of God's Kingdom order.

4) **ORDINANCES**: Colossians 2:20, *"Wherefore if ye be dead with Christ from the rudiments of the world, why, as though living in the world, are ye subject to* **ordinances***,"* (emphases added). Nelson's Three-in-One Bible Reference defines this word as *"regulation established for proper procedure."*[67] The Strong's Exhaustive Concordance Greek Word for ordinances in this scripture is # 1379 *"dogmatizō"* – "to prescribe by statute, i.e. (reflectively) to submit to ceremonial rule."[68] It comes from the Greek root # 1378, meaning 'law (civil, ecclesiastical (religious) or ceremonial) decrees or regulations".[69] The scripture is asking, why, if we are dead with Christ to the traditions and principles (rudiments) of the world, do we still live our lives in according to our cultures ceremonial rules or regulations (ordinances)? For the Hebrew who accepted Christ, the question was, why were they still performing the ceremonial rules and regulations of the Old Covenant, the old way of worship. I would therefore also ask many of my Christian brothers and sisters of today this question - why would we still practice the old religion after we accepted Jesus into our lives as our Lord and Savior? Why would we consider the old ways as the more important law by believing and following them instead of God's Word?

Upon accepting Christ we must fully embrace the work of the Cross in every area of our lives. I will be so bold as to say that we must even die to our traditions, if they stand between Jesus and us. Following tradition hinders us from truly being all that God has called us to be. We are not called to follow our traditions. Instead, we are called to follow Christ and to walk in His ways.

"But now, after ye have known God, or rather have been known of God, how turn ye again to the weak and beggarly elements, whereunto ye desire to be in bondage?" (Galatians 4:9). These elements by which we are held are fetishes, ornaments, traditions, dances and ceremonies. They are described as being *"weak and beggarly"*. In other words they have no point and they lack what we truly need. They are empty of any reality of Christ. At one time they meant a great deal to many of us, because we put our whole faith in these items - a false faith in things such as: sweet grass, sweat lodges, potlatches, totem poles, dream catchers, medicine bags, sage, medicine men/women, shamans, symbolic items, pipe ceremonies, sun dances, spirit dances, drum dances and other supposed helps to our spiritual life. It was all we knew before knowing Christ. We must be reminded that **these hold us in bondage and keep us from true freedom.** They hinder us from truly knowing our Heavenly Father and having a clear revelation of who He is and His true purpose for our lives. These cultural elements distract us and bring us down a path of deception and loss. We think we know the truth, but instead, we are confused because

we are mixing our old religion with the Word of God. If we truly knew the truth, we wouldn't have to mix religions; we would follow the one true and living way. Jesus said, "*I am the way, the truth and the life, no man cometh unto the Father but by me.*" (John 14:6)

It is through Jesus that we find our answers. It is through Jesus that we can come to the Father, our Creator. It is through Jesus that we receive life and wholeness. He was not in bondage nor was He subject to the traditions of the culture that surrounded Him as He walked on the earth. Although He did eat with sinners, He did not partake in their sin. He spoke with the woman at the well and revealed himself to her without joining her in worship at the mountain of her fathers in order to win her over to His Kingdom. He transcended His culture and His times. When taken to Jerusalem as a 12 year old boy to celebrate the Passover, He spent three days amongst the teachers stating to His parents that He was about His Father's business. As an adult He celebrated the Passover with His disciples and through it prepared them for His death as the Spotless Lamb of God. He was not bound by the prevailing culture. His very life and teaching often went against many of the traditions of that time. He called the tradition-bound Pharisees and Sadducees "hypocrites". He was constantly rebuking them because they questioned His words and pressured Him to conform to their ways. I have never found Jesus compromising in the Scriptures.

We should ask ourselves, "*Is my adherence to 'culture' keeping me from a right relationship with*

God and a full revelation of Him?" We can only receive a full revelation of the Father though Jesus His Son as revealed in the written Word of God. We also need to ask, "*Is my devotion to culture distorting or keeping me from a true perception of God?*" Remember, looking to things in our culture cannot help us perceive God; only God's Word and His Holy Spirit will give us true perception of who He is. Another question we may ask is, "*Are the strongholds of spiritual darkness broken in my life?*" As the light of His Word enters our hearts we will truly see His truth and His truth will set us free. Finally let us honestly ask, "*Have I fully surrendered to the work of the Cross?*" The Cross will bring death to self and His life will come forth in us instead.

Our faith must be in God rather than in "religious performance". Our fleshly goals, ways of life, mind sets, traditions, beliefs and values must bow to the Lordship of Jesus. They must be taken to the cross and they must die there. In other words, we must recognize that our own efforts are not the key to eternal life. The Cross must be applied to every aspect of our lives, culture, and lifestyle. There is no other way to true life except through Jesus Christ (John 14:6). The benefit of allowing our old ways to die at the foot of the Cross is that Jesus gives us life in exchange. What an incredible deal! His life and resurrection power comes forth in us when we let go of our old ways and sources of ungodly power. Religion and tradition are not able to do this for us. They keep us in bondage, but Christ made it possible for you and me to have this freedom!

"Stand fast therefore in the liberty wherewith Christ hath made us free, and be not entangled again with the yoke of bondage" (Galatians 5:1) If we go back, if we compromise even a little by putting our faith in the elements of our culture and then begin using the elements of our culture to accomplish what God Himself would do in and through us, we entangle ourselves again in bondage. As stated earlier, native sacraments have spiritual ties in the spirit world. Once we have been freed from these spiritual ties, we must not go back to them again. Remember, it is the person who has been made free not the object. Just because a person has been freed from the power of darkness, does not mean that the sacrament will not affect him again if he continues to hold on to it. Indeed, it will bring him back into bondage because he is actually agreeing with spirits that are not of God. ***Agreeing with Christ and with what Christ has done for us at the cross brings liberty.***

> *"If then you have been raised with Christ, keep looking for the good things of heaven. This is where Christ is seated on the right side of God. Keep your minds thinking about things in heaven. Do not think about things on the earth. You are dead to the things of this world. Your new life is now hidden in God through Christ."* (Colossians 3:1-3).[70]

III) *ASK FOR GOD'S WISDOM "IF ANY OF YOU LACK WISDOM LET HIM ASK OF GOD..."*

(JAMES 1:5)

After reviewing the previous scriptures, we must ask this important question:

Does this mean we are to remain secluded from relating with people outside our Church walls? Yes and no. One dear Native Christian lady was faced with a decision whether she would attend a supper that followed a funeral service. Her fellow Native Christian friend with her left the building with a self-righteous attitude that she would not eat a meal with those that blessed food to the spirits of the dead. The lady did not follow her friend, instead she stayed with the people in order to offer them comfort in their time of grief. She was relieved to find that night, that the food for the supper was not offered to the ancestral spirits. She prayed inwardly asking the Lord for what she should do and she felt led by the Lord to remain with the bereaved family.

Traditions of cultural practice within the religious beliefs of each society should never take precedent over God's Kingdom order or His Word. However, we always need to be led by the Spirit of God, especially when faced with the question of being involved in certain settings. Where God has placed each of us is our sphere of influence. The world, with all its multi-cultural aspects, should not influence God's people, rather God's people are to impact and influence the society in which they live.

In one incident our team was invited to a potlatch (a memorial-feast). A particular singing group was not able to attend due to weather conditions. We were asked to take their place and to sing a certain hymn that had been chosen for the unveiling of the tombstone. Following the feast, the community would then proceed to the longhouse to continue the memorial with the giving and receiving of gifts, along with ceremonial rituals, and sacred songs sung along with the sacred drum. What were we to do? Were we to tell them this was not of God and we would have nothing to do with the devil's works of darkness? I think not! First, we went to God in prayer. Our leader felt the Lord would have our team sing the hymn as this would be our opportunity to share His life with the grieving family. By the same token, we did not feel to go with the rest of the community to the longhouse. Instead, we spent the night in prayer for the people of the village. As we held the prayer meeting, there were others from the community who had not attended the feast who came and joined our prayer meeting. They did not feel they should attend the traditional ceremonies in the longhouse either. Our team did not say that the Christians should not go there, and we did not tell anyone what to do. When the believers realized that we were not going to the longhouse, they were excited that there was an alternative and joined us in prayer for their people.

A fellow minister related to me the story of when she and her ministry team were ministering in a village that was deeply rooted in their cultural and religious traditions. She had been asked to perform a wedding ceremony and the rest of the team was also invited to attend the wedding. There was one problem: just before the wedding they decided to change the location of the wedding ceremony to their sacred circle, where they would "feed the fire". Rather than refusing to participate, she went to prayer and asked the Lord for direction. She felt released in her spirit to still perform the wedding ceremony. She asked the bride and groom-to-be, if they would like the ministry team to bring their instruments and play music while people waited for the wedding party to arrive. They agreed that this would be a nice thing to do. The team prepared themselves in prayer and believed that God would be sovereign enough to touch the hearts of the people. On the day of the wedding, the bride and groom were an hour and a half late, so the team filled the entire time with songs that were sung at gospel tent meetings. One woman was angry at that minister and the team with her. She asked if it was an open wedding as they would be "feeding the fire". The minister said that she had been asked to do the wedding. At the same time, others were calling out requests for their favorite hymns. Suddenly the presence of God filled the area. As the wedding began, and the scripture was read, peace settled in so much that, the dogs stopped barking, the restless children were no longer restless and tears flowed down the faces of some of the people of the crowd. After the wedding ceremony was performed, the team went home and a sudden storm came. It rained so hard that they had a very wet, fizzled out "feeding of the fire" ceremony. God was definitely sovereign in this situation and the people witnessed it.

These examples are not written to suggest they should be imitated. The principle here is that we must seek direction *from the Lord*. If He does not permit us to do something, it is because He knows what lies ahead. If He does give permission, then He is sovereign enough to take care of the details. The key is to be led by His Spirit as it states in Romans 8:14, 16, *"For as many are led by the Spirit of God, they are the sons of God…The Spirit itself bears witness with our spirit…"* The word *"sons"* in this context of scripture speaks of *maturity*. We, as His children, grow in relationship with Him; as we grow, we learn to hear His voice more clearly, for Jesus said in John 10:27 that His sheep hear His voice, He knows us and we follow Him, and that another voice we will not follow. This speaks of a close walk with the Lord, so close that we know His voice and anything else is strange to us. Job 32:8 states, *"But there is a spirit in man: and the inspiration of the Almighty giveth them understanding."* If we sincerely seek the Lord, He will give His wisdom in each situation and show us what to do. It is important to know what you are dealing with and also to know the Word of God and to heed His voice.

Earlier I mentioned an example of protocol. I would like to relate another example of protocol: the giving of tobacco. A lady related to me a practice that often takes place in her field of work. Her office firm was planning a special dinner which they would be hosting. They were required to invite those they considered to be elders in their culture. The protocol in this setting was to honor the elders by giving them a pouch of tobacco. Doing so meant that you looked to the elders for wisdom and counsel and that you acknowledged the sacrifices they had made. An elder is either one who is a medicine man/woman or one who is at least very well practiced in Native religion and traditions. In this incident, the lady related to me that during the planning meeting her co-workers wanted to initiate her so she could give the tobacco to the elder they had invited. There was only one problem: this lady did not practice Native religion even though her heritage is Cree First Nations. She is a Christian. Realizing the implications, she felt she could not partake in this little ritual. By participating, she would be saying that she agreed with the belief that is embedded in this practice - that she needed the native elder to cover her and to give her counsel. Her personal conviction was in accordance with the Word of God, that Jesus paid the final sacrifice to be her covering and that the Holy Spirit was her counselor as given in John 15:26. A co-worker of hers who was a part of this planning committee, who also was a Native Christian, did not take this practice seriously but rather took it lightly. "Its just protocol!" she stated to the first lady. However, the first lady, realizing what the implications were, would not take it lightly. She looked to God for wisdom and God granted it to her. She shared with the planning committee that she did not want to participate in this ritual because she did not practice Native religion. She asked if they could they choose someone else; if not, could she give a blanket instead of tobacco. The difference between giving a blanket and giving tobacco is significant. A blanket given as a gift usually meant that you were saying "thank you". Giving tobacco usually meant that you were saying, "I acknowledge you as my spiritual leader and covering". It is important to understand that protocol cannot be taken lightly. It is important to know the significance of what you are participating in and most of all to rely on God's wisdom, and to know what His Word says. Inspite of the pressure to conform, do not compromise your standards. The situation this lady was in at her job was not easy. She did pray in her heart for God's wisdom as to how to co-operate with her co-workers. I believe God granted it to her.

We must be sure that we do not misrepresent Him, whether in compromise of our Biblical standards or through legalistic preaching. Both are mistakes that have taken place in the history of the church at large. It is wisest to stick to lifting up Jesus and Him alone. To preach with legalistic mindsets is simply to drive people further away from the Gospel. Even if they are not driven away, often all you have is conformation instead of transformation because legalism only causes one to conform to its rules. Jesus alone can truly transform us. Jesus would rather have us a transformed people who know Him, His Word and His ways. A few years back as I was before the Lord in prayer, He spoke into my spirit, "*I do not want my people to conform...*" I thought, what do you mean, Lord? He then said, "*I want them to be transformed.*"

That is what Christianity is. It is a transformation of the heart that causes everything else in our lives to line up with His way of life. Romans 12:2 tells us that we are to be transformed by the renewing of our minds. Ezekiel 36:26, 27 also tells us that He will give us a new heart and He will put His Spirit within us and cause us to walk in His statutes. Statutes mean ordinances, laws, precepts and such. In other words, we begin to walk in His ways, not our ways. If there is no inward transformation upon receiving Christ, then it is easy to conform to another way, whatever that way is.

I was with a ministry team in a particular village (I will not indicate where in order to protect the people) where a missionary had lived many years before. He had shared the Gospel of Jesus with them and preached against their traditions. He told the people that their regalia and carvings were evil; therefore, they should get rid of them. The people responded with honest hearts. After the missionary left, the people discovered a few years later, that he had hidden their carvings and ceremonial regalia underneath the church basement and sold each item to a museum for large sums of money. This was grievous not only to the people but also to God's heart. First of all, the Lord had been misrepresented, and secondly, the people reacted by going back to their former traditions. Today they will accept evangelists who visit them, but Jesus is no longer first in many of their lives. Now a major revitalization of culture has taken place within this particular community to the point that it has taken precedent over their faith in

Jesus. Many feel ripped off by religion, and because of this, they feel they do not need Jesus. How sad! This case is one of many examples of the effect of legalistic preaching. Yet still, within this community, there have been some individuals who shared with us, that in spite of this incident, they know that Jesus is the *only* way and they refuse to turn back to their former traditions, even though they are shunned by their own people. That takes a lot of courage!

We are not the Holy Spirit. It is *His* job to do the convicting (see John17:6-10), not ours. God is big enough to speak to each individual about what is acceptable and what is not in their lives. I am living proof of that! If you are prone to legalistic preaching you need to pray for God's love and compassion to fill your heart with His grace for the ones you are ministering to. "*For God did not send His Son into the world to condemn the world; but that the world through him might be saved*" (John 3:17).

Legalism is not the only ditch we must avoid when looking to God for wisdom in dealing with cultural issues. Man's way has often been to react to legalism and to do the opposite. However, to do the opposite, preaching redemption of culture, is to lay a wrong foundation and true repentance is not understood. I have witnessed this over and over again in the different communities I have been to. Many times Jesus was simply added on as another god. For example, some will pray to the eagle, speak to the ravens and use "healing stones" in Jesus' name. Talk about syncretism at its "finest"! When faced with such incidences it is tempting to address it with legalistic preaching. If we start to do this, we then walk in our own wisdom and a religious spirit will try to creep into our hearts. Conversely, for others these things are accepted and as long as Jesus is in there somewhere, "all is well". Because of this confusion many do not live for the Lord. Some get lost in the shuffle and others get lost in defending their position rather than ministering Jesus. We need to pray for *God's* wisdom when faced with these issues wherever we go. It takes humility to minister the Gospel and we must operate out of God's love. Yes, His word says in Isaiah 45:5, "*I am the Lord and there is none else, there is no God beside me…*" but we must continually **point them to Jesus,** and pray for the individuals who are "mixing" and <u>allow God</u> to speak to their hearts. This is how God used key Christian leaders in my life. They did not condone what I believed or practiced, but neither did they condemn me. All I recall is that each one would simply say, "*Keep on loving Jesus and stay close to Him. God will teach you from His Word.*" That takes real faith!

PART SIX

WORSHIP

I) *"THE KEY TO WORSHIP"*

In John chapter four we read that as Jesus sat at the well while His disciples went to town to shop for food, He saw a woman there and began to talk with her. The woman, was a Samaritan. In her day, Jews and Samaritans did not associate with each other. The Jews of that day believed they were superior to other races and Jewish men did not sit and talk with women, especially gentile women. In that part of the story she asked Jesus why He was talking to her, especially in public, as He was a Jew and she was a Samaritan. This was totally against the cultural norms of the day. As we have stated earlier, Jesus was not bound by tradition. His desire was to reveal Himself to her because He perceived the spiritual hunger deep within her heart. He went on to show her that He was the source of living water from which her spiritual thirst could truly be satisfied. Both the woman and Jesus knew she had been from one relationship to another with many men (John 4:18). Yet, as Jesus looked past her sin and continued speaking with her, she began to ask for the water which He spoke of that caused people to never thirst again. Through this encounter He was able to meet her real need and she, as well as many from her village, came to know the love and mercy of God.

Let us now look at the account of the woman at the well and her conversation with Jesus regarding the issue of worship.

"The woman saith unto Him, Sir, I perceive that thou art a prophet. Our fathers worshipped in this mountain; and ye say, that in Jerusalem is the place where men ought to worship. Jesus saith unto her, Woman, believe me, the hour cometh, when ye shall neither in this mountain, nor yet at Jerusalem, worship the Father. Ye worship ye know not what: we know what we worship: for salvation is of the Jews. But the hour cometh, and now is, when the true worshippers shall worship the Father in spirit and in truth: for the Father seeketh such to worship him. God is a Spirit: and they that worship him must worship him in spirit and in truth. The woman saith unto him, I know that Messiah cometh, which is called Christ: when he is come, he will tell us all things. Jesus saith unto her, I that speak unto thee am he." John 4:19-26

Here we see two forms of worship. The mountain, which is where the Samaritans worshipped, is symbolic of one form; Jerusalem is symbolic of another. The underlying question that this woman had was: Which is the right way? Why did Jesus reply first of all by saying that her people did not know what they worshiped and His people did and then proceed to say that salvation was of the Jews? That is an interesting statement. It sounds biased? Well, not so when you look at things from God's perspective.

God's concern is the souls of mankind. He had chosen the nation of Israel to serve Him and to be a light to the world by which all men would know that the way to God was through the blood of the Lamb. It was God who authorized the formation of the Jewish religion, if you want to call it that. Yet, it was not religion that He wanted from man. When you read through the books of Exodus, Leviticus and Deuteronomy you will find that God was very particular in how His people were to approach Him. If one "jot or title" was out of place, they fell short of His glory. God was, in effect, showing the Jews that if they wanted to be at peace with Him then they would have to come to Him *His way*. This was humanly impossible, for as the Word clarifies, that to offend the law in one area means you have offended the whole law (see James 2:10). Mankind, as a whole, needs to understand that it is impossible to please God by religious duties and rituals. These things may please flesh, but they do not please God! God's intent for man is that man must recognize that he is indeed a sinner and is in need of God's mercy. That is why He sent Jesus the Messiah, as the Lamb of God, to be the final sacrifice for our sin.

Jesus also said that the mountain or Jerusalem will not be the place of worship. Why? Everything was about to change. He goes on further to say that *"the hour cometh and NOW IS"*; He was speaking of Himself as the one who would pay the price for our sin. Hebrews 10:22 tells us that without the shedding of blood there is no remission of sins – meaning forgiveness. The way to God is through the blood of the Lamb. That is what the Jewish people understood. Yet, the blood of the lamb slain on the Day of Atonement, in Jerusalem, was only a covering for their sin. However, now Jesus had come and was about to be crucified on the cross at Calvary where He would become the final sacrifice as the Lamb of God, doing more than covering our sin, but instead, taking it away. His blood does just that! His blood cleanses us from all unrighteousness and we are made new creatures! It was for all mankind, not just for those who believed in the atonement sacrifice offered in Jerusalem.

Jesus was telling the woman that because of His death for all, neither form of worship would be necessary; both would be obsolete, whether on "this mountain or at Jerusalem" - those that worship Him will worship Him in spirit and in truth. The only way to come before God is through the Blood of Christ. We worship Him because He has washed our sins away. **He becomes our focus, instead of our forms of worship! When our forms of worship, what-**

ever they may be, become the focus then we have missed the mark, just as the Jews did. One author states,

> *"Frankly, the music style you like best says more about you – your background and personality – than it does about God. ...We worship to bring pleasure for God's benefit. When we worship, our goal is to bring pleasure to God, not ourselves."*[71]

God is after our hearts, not our forms of worship. Christ is the focus and in worshipping Him we express that worship as human beings, whether we are Native, German, French, Italian, Greek, Hispanic, Ukrainian, African, Chinese, Scottish, Irish, Italian or Englishmen, etc. **It is not a form or expression we have learned from this world, but rather it comes forth by the Spirit of God as we worship Him with all our heart.**

We worship Christ for <u>who He is</u> and not for who <u>we</u> are. It is about Him, not us. That is the key to worship. *"Forasmuch as ye know that ye were not redeemed with corruptible things, as silver and gold, from vain conversation received by tradition from your fathers; But with the precious blood of Christ, as of a lamb without blemish and spot: Who verily was foreordained before the foundation of the world, but was manifest in these last times for you, Who by Him do believe in God, that raised him up from the dead, and gave Him glory; that your faith and hope might be in God"* (I Peter 1:18-21). The conversation received by tradition from our fathers is what we have been taught by oral tradition. If the word of God calls it vain- meaning: useless; conceited; empty; to no end[72] – then why are we trying to redeem it? It goes on further to say that Christ was sent that our faith and our hope might be in God. This does not say that our faith and our hope might be in our traditions, or money or anything else of this world. The New Life Bible states from I Peter 1:18-21,

> *"You know you were not bought and made free from sin by paying gold or silver which comes to an end. And you know you were not saved from the punishment of sin by the way of life that you were given from your early fathers. That way of life was worth nothing. The blood of Christ saved you. This blood is of great worth and no amount of money can buy it. Christ was given as a lamb without sin and without spot. Long before the world was made, God chose Christ, to be given to you in these last days. Because of Christ, you have put your trust in God. He raised Christ from the dead and gave Him the great honor. So now your faith and hope are in God."* (I Peter 1:18-21).[73]

The traditions of old are worth nothing in comparison to the Blood of Christ which is our only hope of salvation, healing and deliverance. The simplicity of our faith does not rest in our form of worship or cultural expressions, but rather, it is in our God.

Before accepting Christ as our Savior, we had a form and a way of doing things. Accepting Christ does not mean that He accommodates Himself to our ways of doing things, rather, we are the ones who change. He transforms all that we are as we become His people. (See again II Corinthians 5:17).

II) *GLORIFYING GOD*

I was engaged in a conversation with a friend of mine concerning the topic of culture. She commented, *"Culture is normally the most common dictator of our society"* This statement never left me. It became clear to me that if anything should be the most common dictator in our personal lives, it ought to be the Word of God. His Word is the final authority. Our lives must line up with His Word in all that we say, think, or do. Joshua 1:8 tells us to meditate on His word day and night; then our way will be prosperous and we will have good success. The Word of God is our ultimate guideline and answer for how we conduct ourselves. God is glorified when we live our lives as He has shown us in His Word.

When it comes to the practical things, how can we know whether we are truly glorifying God or not? One must reflect, *"Is what I am presenting glorifying God, or self, or some other deity?"* We need to know that there is a deceiver out there, Satan, who is ready to devour us with his lies. John 10:10 informs us that Satan comes to steal, kill, and to destroy. He uses religious ceremonial practices, twisting and perverting them, to divert us from a true relationship with our

Father. The focus shifts then from a living relationship with God to dead ceremonies and practices that make up our traditional values and belief systems. Superstition supersedes true faith in God and we start to participate in ceremonies that worship the creation, idols, and false gods. Our motivation is no longer a love for God, but a fear of the unknown, a desire to appease wrathful demonic forces. Remember: *God motivates by love, not fear*. The woman at the well was motivated by His love as she encountered Jesus that day.

Inherently, we know that we are born to worship; but, what will we worship? Worship is often defined as affection towards something or someone. There is an innate desire to release that affection toward God our Creator. Glorifying God is something we were born to do. Referring back to John 4:24, notice it states, "…*in Spirit and in truth*". You can be led by the Spirit, and the Spirit will never contradict His Word. John 4:24 from the Amplified Bible, reads in this manner, "*God is a Spirit (a spiritual being) and those who worship Him must worship Him in Spirit and in Truth (reality)*." God becomes a living reality to you.

Ephesians 1:4 states, "*According as He has chosen us in Him before the foundation of the world, that we should be holy and without blame before Him in love*." There is a tendency to think that God called us on the day we became Christian; but, the Bible says we were chosen before this world was made. Next we see what He chose us, "…*to be holy and without blame before Him in love*." How is that possible since we always fall short? Ephesians 1:7 states, *"In whom we have redemption through His blood, the forgiveness of sins, according to the riches of His grace;"* It is only through the blood of Christ that we can be holy and without blame before God and it is done by His love. Redemption comes only through the blood of Christ. His blood was not just shed for our sins; but that we might receive the forgiveness of sins and so be redeemed. Then out of a response to His love for us, we worship Him.

In our fallen, corrupted, and unredeemed state we can not worship God in spirit and in truth, because we are bound by sin, the law, the traditions of men, and death. Nothing we do through cultural means, by tradition or by law will bring life to us, nor will it glorify God. Whether we want to admit it or not, our culture often is an idol. Culture can become a hindrance in our relationship with our Creator. We need to be more willing to lay aside our culture in order to have greater fellowship with our Lord. There comes a time when culture is of little value to us because God is more important than our traditions and our native identity or our non-native identity. Anything apart from the redemption of His blood is under a curse. Galatians 3:13 states, *"Christ hath redeemed us from the curse of the law, being made a curse for us:..."*. Christ redeemed us in order that we can live as true worshippers and as His children. We, as His children, bring Him glory, because, as His children, we worship our Creator in Spirit and in Truth. *"Having predestined us unto the adoption of children by Jesus Christ to himself, according to the good pleasure of his will, To the praise of the glory of his grace, wherein he hath made us accepted in the beloved.*" (Ephesians 1:5, 6). *We* are destined to glorify God with our very lives; yet, **without Christ** we cannot do it. Christ in us changes our way of life and causes us to worship Him in Spirit and in Truth. It is Christ that forms us into His image. He is the image of God and His Spirit dwells within us. His nature lives through us. We read the statement, "*Let us make man in our image*" (Genesis 1:6). We were destined to be made in the image of God, but it is *sin* that hinders our growth.

Therefore, as Hebrews 12:1 states, "*…let us lay aside every weight, and the sin with doth so easily beset us…*" What does it mean to truly lay aside every weight? What are the weights that hinder our spiritual growth in Christ? What kind of sin(s) hinders us from genuinely experiencing the true worship of our Creator, Jesus Christ? These are questions one must consider and ask the Holy Spirit of God to reveal in order to further our spiritual growth in Him. I John1:9 states, "*If we confess our sins, he is faithful and just to forgive us our sins, and to cleanse us from all unrighteousness.*"

We were born to bear spiritual fruit. "*Of his own will, begat he us with the Word of truth, that we should be a kind of first fruits of his creatures*" (James 1:18). Our salvation experience is more than being forgiven at the Cross; it is an actual re-birthing within us. We are no longer spiritually dead; we have been made alive unto God! "*And you hath He quickened, who were dead in trespasses and sins;*" (Ephesians 2:1).

The true part of us, our spirit, is made alive unto God! That is a miraculous event! His Spirit now dwells in us and His Spirit begins to form His nature in us, as we grow closer to Him. The increasing nature of God in us is seen in the fruit of the Spirit mentioned in Galatians 5:22-23. This fruit develops in us, as we grow closer to Him. As we grow, God begins to deal with the things in our lives that stunt our spiritual growth. "*But after the kindness and love of God and our Savior toward man appeared, Not by works of righteousness which we have done, but according to his mercy he saved us, by the washing of regeneration, and renewing of the Holy Ghost*" (Titus 3:4,5).

Regarding cultural living, we can ask the following questions: "*Does cultural practice bring more fruit of the Spirit, or, am I relying on carnal things for a more meaningful walk with God? Does the exercise of my cultural traditions hinder me from growing in Him and truly experiencing the things of God? How can I truly worship God in spirit and in truth as Jesus said?*" It is important to ponder these questions, as they will challenge each of us to seek after God with all our heart.

III) *WHAT DOES GOD HONOR?*

Let us now carefully consider two characters in the Bible. They are Cain and Abel, the first two sons of Adam and Eve. The issue at hand here is *what does God honor?*

"And Adam knew Eve His wife; and she conceived, and bare Cain, and said, I have begotten a man from the Lord. And again she bore his brother Abel. And Abel was a keeper of the sheep, but Cain was a tiller of the ground. And in the process of time it came to pass, that Cain brought of the fruit of the ground offering it unto the Lord. And Abel, he also brought of the firstlings of his flock and of the fat thereof. And the Lord had respect unto Abel and to his offering. But unto Cain, to his offering he had no respect. And Cain was very wroth, and his countenance fell. And the Lord said unto Cain, Why art thou wroth? And why is thy countenance fallen? If thou doest well, shalt thou not be accepted? And if thou doest not well, sin lieth at the door. And unto thee shall be his desire, and thou shalt rule over him" (Genesis 4:1-7).

In these early days, God initiated a sacrificial system for mankind in order that man could maintain relationship with Him. A lamb without spot or blemish had to be sacrificed and burned on an altar unto the Lord as an offering for their sins; in this way, God would cover their sin. This system later became an institution and was set up as a picture of the coming of Jesus Christ, who was the true sacrifice for forgiveness of sin. The precedent for this was seen when God Himself shed blood and clothed Adam and Eve with the skins of the slain animals.

He covered them from the shame of their sin HIS WAY!

Cain, as a tiller of the ground, came to make his sacrifice unto the Lord by taking the fruit of the ground and then offering it to the Lord. Notice that he did not offer a lamb without spot or blemish. God replied to this by rejecting Cain's offering. Abel was a keeper of the sheep and when he went to make his sacrifice of a lamb, God had respect for Abel's offering. God was not playing favorites. As Acts 10:24 tells us, God is no respecter of persons. Why then did God not respect Cain's offering when, after all, it was his best fruit? The principle here is simple. The reason God did not respect or honor Cain's offering was that it was an offering of his own choosing. Cain did not respect what God required of him and gave the work of his own hands. Today this would be like our own works. It would have been better for Cain to purchase a spotless lamb from his brother Abel with his fruit and then sacrifice the lamb to God, as God had required. By doing things his own way, Cain actually rejected the ways of God and in rejecting God's ways, he rejected God Himself; therefore God rejected Him. Proverbs 3:5 and 6 advises us *"Trust in the Lord with all thine heart; and lean not unto thine own understanding. In all thy ways acknowledge him, and he shall direct thy paths."*

Jesus came as the Lamb, the Final Sacrifice that paid for all the sins of the whole world for all eternity. When we reject Jesus, we are rejecting the Creator who made a way for us to get to Him. How do we reject Jesus, God's provision? Often we do this by trying to do things our own way through man-made forms of religious worship and ritualistic tradition. Here is where we fall short. We try to use our own works to reach God. Using our own efforts is our way of saying that we can get to the Creator some way other than meeting His requirements. We devise our own way instead of choosing God's way. In other words, we are leaning on our own understanding and in so doing we do not acknowledge the ways of God. This is a horrible thing to do because we are rejecting the provision God made for our spiritual cleansing through the shed blood of Jesus. If God did not accept Cain's sacrifice then what makes us think He will accept ours? We are not exempt. God will not honor our independent ways of sacrifice. That is false religion. We enter a proper and right standing relationship with our Creator only through Jesus.

IV) *WHAT PLEASES GOD*

What was it that pleased God so much about Abel's offering? It was his humble and submissive act of obedience; yet, most of all it was *his faith*. He trusted God so much that he was willing to do whatever God required of him in offering the sacrifice. Hebrew 11:6 tells us that we cannot please God without faith.

Ephesians 2:8, 9 states, *"It is by grace that we are saved through faith; and THAT NOT OF YOURSELVES: it is the gift of God: NOT OF WORKS, lest any man should boast,"* (emphasis added). Faith in Christ is looking to Him as the only one who can reconcile us to God. God is a God of relationship; He wants us to know Him personally. Faith in Him is reliance upon *Him*, not our own works. As we rely more and more on Him, the fruitfulness of the Holy Spirit will develop in our lives. When we rely on our own way of doing things, it hinders our spiritual growth and stunts the growth of spiritual fruit.

Learning to depend on Him takes a total surrender of all that we are. As stated in Joshua 1:8, we are to meditate on His Word day and night so that we can learn to do all according to what is written in His Word. Why? That we might be prosperous and have good success. The Word is His truth. The Truth is His light. "*Thy Word is a lamp unto my feet, and light unto my path*" (Psalm 119:105). We must allow His light to shine in every area of our lives to expose any deception that we are walking in. As stated earlier, what we do must line up with His Word. Anything in our culture that causes us to rely on traditions and man-made forms of worship to reach our Creator is wrong. Instead, we need to rely solely on what Christ did for us at the Cross and to worship Him in spirit and in truth from that place.

As we all know, light reveals. The more we study His word, the more the truth of His Word exposes any and every darkness. God wants us to walk in truth. Walking in truth gradually leads to worshipping the Creator in spirit and in truth. Our own fleshly efforts are carnal and not of faith. Our own fleshly efforts are self-deception and not truth. In John 16:13, we have the promise of God's Spirit to guide us into all truth and to teach us all things. Because He wants us to walk in truth, He sends the Holy Spirit to teach us how to worship Him in spirit and in truth, so we may know Him and become more like Him. *It is not rituals and traditions that we need.* It is <u>faith in God</u> and <u>knowing Jesus</u>. As we enter into a closer relationship with God, our love for Him becomes so strong that our lives begin to line up with His Word; we serve Him to please Him because of that love.

> *"And we know that the Son of God is come, and hath given us an understanding, that we may know him that is true, and we are in him that is true, even in his Son Jesus Christ. This is the true God and eternal life. Little children, keep yourselves from idols. Amen"* I John 5:20

CONCLUSION

"For I am not ashamed of the Gospel of Christ: for it is the power of God unto salvation to everyone that believeth; to the Jew first, and also to the Greek. For therein is the righteousness of God revealed from faith to faith: as it written, the just shall live by faith." Romans 1:16-17

The <u>Gospel</u> is the *power of God* unto salvation, not the mixing, nor any cultural aspects of whatever group we are from. The <u>Gospel</u> is for the *salvation* of everyone who **believes**. It is the <u>Gospel</u> of Christ that provides us with God's guidelines and teaches us not only the way of salvation but also how to worship and how to live in God's freedom. Will "mixing" set people free from the bonds of wickedness and death? No! Christ sets people free. Christ redeems those within a culture and takes them out of the old pattern of living and teaches them a new and holy way of life. Paul stated in Galatians 5:11, *"And I brethren, if I yet preach circumcision, why do I suffer persecution? Then is the offense of the cross ceased."* Paul was pressured to teach the Gentile believers to carry on with the old traditions of the Jews and mix them with faith in Christ. He strongly urged that circumcision was no longer necessary as Jesus was enough. Paul, in his day, faced the same kind of deception as we do today with syncretism. It was the same deceiving spirit that lurked among the Christians of that day that lurks among the Body of Christ in our day. Again he states, *"For Christ sent me not to baptize, but to preach the gospel: not with wisdom of words, lest the cross of Christ should be made of none effect, For the preaching of the cross is to them foolishness; but unto us which are saved it is the power of God."* (I Corinthians 1:17-18)

A miracle takes place in one's life when a person believes the Gospel message that Jesus died for his/her sin; that Jesus was buried and rose again on the third and glorious day. That person becomes born again and a new relationship with the Father begins. **The key to continuing in this relationship is to stay focused on Jesus and to meditate on His Word.** As we continue in His Word, (not our tradi- tions) Jesus said we are His disciples, indeed, and we shall know the truth and the truth shall make us free (John 8:31-32).

Ezekiel 36:25-27 states, *"Then will I sprinkle clean water upon you, and ye shall be clean: from all your filthiness, and from all your idols, will I cleanse you. A new heart will I give you, and a new spirit will*

I put within you: and I will take away the stony heart out of your flesh, and I will give you an heart of flesh. And I will put my spirit within you, and cause you to walk in my statutes, and ye shall keep my judgments, and do them." As God's people, we no longer follow the religious traditions of our ancestors but we walk in the statutes of God. He determines our values, our beliefs, and our purpose in life. If there is anything good in us it is from God, not from our ancestors' traditions, nor from our own abilities (See James 1:17).

As a people we need to know our Creator in the person of Jesus Christ as our personal Lord and Savior. As Christians our identity is found in Christ, and without Christ, cultural identity means nothing. It is good to know who you are as a person and to have dignity as native person; but, if you esteem that above identifying with Christ, it is of no value. If you do not know Jesus as your personal Lord and Savior and are not filled with His Spirit, you will never find fulfillment. Jesus sees our brokenness and our pain and if we will come to the cross and give Him our burdens, He will sustain us. He will give us the power to overcome the world with all its temptations and to have joy everlasting!

In the section on "Syncretism-Mixing" we touched on the Ephesian church as described in Acts 19. In Revelations 2:1-7, the church of Ephesus was given a letter from Christ through the apostle John in his latter years. Jesus' message was that He knew their works and labor of love, that they had not tolerated false teachers within their midst and had proven them to be liars. Yet, their tireless labor in their work for His Kingdom caused them to wane in their love for Him. He called them to return to their first love. <u>He</u> was their first love. "*But this thou hast, that thou hatest the deeds of the Nicolaitans, which I also hate.*" (Revelations 2:6). Now where did this come from? Who were the Nicolaitans? What were their deeds? The Nicolaitans were an early Christian heretical sect made up of followers of Nicolas and were compared with another heretical group holding the doctrine of Balaam. Some early church leaders believed the Nicolaitans later became a Gnostic sect.[74] The Gnostics were a group who blended Christian teaching with Greek philosophy.[75] They were also causing confusion within the church of Pergamos as mentioned in Revelation 2:12-17. In Pergamos, the believers allowed the doctrine of the Balaam and the doctrine of the Nicolaitans to be taught. This very issue was repulsive to not only the church of Ephesus and Pergamos, but also to the Lord!

Why was He calling the church of Ephesus back to their first love? Why is He calling the church of today back to her first love? The Ephesian church was hard at work for the Lord and labored to share the gospel message of Jesus. By the same token, because of being so busy with laboring for the Lord (instead of spending time with the Lord), they lost their first love. When we lose our first love, it is easy to lose sight of why we do what we do and a religious spirit often takes the place of our first love. We become legalistic and are no longer motivated by the love of God. With this religious spirit of legalism we often either get on the "band wagon" promoting and defending mixing, or we make ourselves enemies of those who are "mixers" instead of being intercessors. James 1:20 states, *"For the wrath of man worketh not the righteousness of God."*

The reason the Lord was calling the church of Ephesus back to their first love was so that His love would begin to fill them afresh and to enable them to touch the hearts of those they reached out to with His love. How much the Lord loves the lost! How much He loves His church! He validated how they felt about the *deeds* of the Nicolaitans by saying that He, too, hated their works; but He did not express hatred toward them as people. If the Ephesians were to really minister to the lost, they needed to be motivated by the love of God and to be led by His Spirit in what God would have them to do. The old saying goes, *"Love the sinner but hate the sin."* We must never forget that we once were sinners, too. When His love motivates us, people respond to His love. No matter where people are at, His love melts away the hardness of hearts and His love draws people to Himself as He begins to reveal Himself to each individual. In this manner He Himself shows the truth of His word. The process of change takes place within the heart of each seeker.

Earlier in this book I mentioned the letter from John to the Laodicean church and the message from Jesus rebuking them for lukewarmness. Lukewarmness also opens the door to syncretism for we often try to accomplish in our flesh what can only be accomplished by seeking the face of God (See II Chronicles

7:14). Lukewarmness or legalism - both have deadly ramifications that affect the Body of Christ and those outside the Body of Christ. **Therefore let us endeavor to truly be lovers of God and not to be lovers of self. Let us endeavor to lift up Jesus.**

In closing, I will share a vision that a young lady from Trinidad had as she was on an outreach with us in Northern Canada. First she saw a large gathering of people; she then saw a person in the front of the crowd lifting up a cross. Those who were right behind this person saw it and began to lift up their own crosses, but those in the back could not see anything; therefore, the lifting up of the cross only went so far. The first person lifted up the cross even higher and soon the lifting up of the cross spread throughout the crowd. The person who first lifted up the cross lifted it up even higher still and soon the whole mass of people, right to the very back, had their crosses raised high. This vision is an important message to us all. Lift up the cross. Lift it high! Lift up the message of Christ and what He did for us on the Cross – this is the Gospel, this is the *GOOD* NEWS! This is what makes the difference!

"Arise, shine; for your light is come, and the glory of the Lord is risen upon thee. For, behold, the darkness shall cover the earth, and gross darkness the people: But the Lord shall arise upon thee, and His glory shall be seen upon thee. And the Gentiles shall come to thy light, and kings to the brightness of thy rising. Lift up thine eyes round about, and

see: all they gather themselves together, they come to thee: thy sons shall come from far, and thy daughters shall be nursed at thy side. Thou shalt see, and flow together, and thine heart shall fear, and be enlarged; because the abundance of the sea shall be converted unto thee, the forces of the Gentiles shall come unto thee." (Isaiah 60:1-5)

APPENDIX:
A

(The following Appendix is a pamphlet given by CHIEF Inc, used with permission by Rev.Huron Claus)

A Biblical Position by Native Leaders on Native Spirituality[1]

Preamble:

Deut. 29:9-12 (NAS)

One of the most critical issues facing the Native Christian Church today is the effort to revive, adapt and utilize Native cultural forms in worship of the church. In the light of the resurgence of Native religious traditionalism, the coming of the peyote movement (Native American Church), the influx

---

[1] CHIEF Inc., *A Biblical Position by Native Leaders on Native Spirituality* (1644 E. Campo Bello Dr. Pheonix AZ 85022: CHIEF Inc. Copyright, 1998) used with permission

of New Age philosophy, and questions concerning Native spirituality and Biblical truth, we as Native believers in Christ, from a score of tribes and with hundreds of combined years of experience in tribal ministry among us, have gathered together to speak with one voice on these subjects to the body of Christ at large, basing our responses on the clear statements of the revealed Word of God.

1Tim. 4:1- 2, 2Tim. 4:3-4, 2Cor. 4:1-2, 1Pet. 4:1.

Our Affirmations:

1. As Native leaders, **we believe** that God the Father, Son and Holy Spirit is personal, eternal, and pre-exists all of creation. God is both the Creator and the Reason for all creation, including the heavens and the earth, plant life, animal life, and man. Life originated from God who is our true heavenly Father, not from earth as our "mother". *Gen. 1:26, Heb. 4:14, Jn. 1:14, 1Tim. 1:17, Jn. 1:1-3, Col. 1:16-17, Neh. 9:6, Rom. 1:20, Acts 17:26-30, Gen. 2:7, Deut. 32:39, Psa. 104:5, Isa. 51:6, Job 12:7-9.*

2. **We believe** that Christ should have preeminence and permeates all aspects of our lives and, through us, all aspects of our cultures, to promote the glory of God. God will not share His glory with anything in creation. To do so is idolatry. To combine elements of Native religion and Biblical truth is syncretism. We must renounce and avoid any form of idolatry and syncretism, because they are forbidden in Scripture. *Deut. 32:39,*

Col. 1:17-19, Eph. 1:6, 12, 14, Heb. 1:3-4, 1Cor. 10:31, Isa. 42:8, Ex. 20:3-6, Rom. 1:23, Col. 3:5, 2Ki. 17:40-41, 2Cor. 6:14-17, 2Cor. 4:2, Acts 19:18-20, 1Cor. 5:11, Isa. 42:17.

3. **We believe** our salvation is in the finished work of Christ and that we cannot add anything to that work to improve our relationship with God. As believers, we should not, therefore, use or attach any spiritual value to items regarded as sacred such as tobacco, cedar smoke, sweet grass, peyote, prayer feathers, fetishes, masks, drums, dances, etc.; to places regarded as sacred such as mother earth, kivas, mountains, sweat lodge, longhouse, or other traditional religious places of worship, etc.; or to spirit beings such as kachinas, skin walkers, animal and nature spirits, etc. *Jn. 19:30, Eph. 2:8-9; 5:8-12, Ex, 20:1-5, Isa. 1:13-16, Deut. 18:9-13, Jn. 4:21-24, Deut. 12:2, 2Chron. 34:4, 1Thes. 1:9.*

4. **We believe** that Christ has always been and always will be the one and the only mediator between God and man. Man is totally helpless to reach God through any traditional spiritual efforts such as Native ceremonies, rituals and forms of worship. *Jn. 14:6, Acts 4:12, 1Tim. 2:5-6, Josh. 24:14-15, Mark 7:1-9, Rom. 3:9-18,23, Col. 2:20-23.*

5. **We believe** we are redeemed and purified only through the blood of Christ for forgiveness of sins and eternal salvation; therefore, we should not teach that a Native can be purified by any other means (smoke, sweats, smudging, other

blood sacrifices, etc.). To do so is to substitute or add Native rituals and ceremonies to the finished work of Christ. *1Pet. 1:18-19, Eph. 1:7, Heb. 9:12-14,22, 1Jn. 1:7, Col. 1:14, Tit. 3:5, Eph. 2:8-9, Col. 2:7-10, Col. 2:20-3:2.*

6. **We believe** that Christ has set us free and that the liberty we have in Christ should not be used as a license to introduce anything from the native traditional ways that would hinder our lives in Christ, that would offend any of our fellow believers, or that would hinder our witness to unbelievers. *Gal. 5:1, Jn. 8:32,36, Gal. 5:13-15, 1Cor. 8, 1Cor. 10:31-33, Rom. 6:16-18.*

7. **We believe** that Christ reigns supreme above all cultures. When Christ redeems and transforms us through faith and obedience to His Word, then Christ will transform our culture through us. (We believe that Christ only redeems people by His blood; the Bible does not teach redemption of culture.) At the same time, we affirm that there are many good traditions within our Native cultures, which enhance the lives of both Christians, and non-Christians. Such traditions include: respect for elders, love for children, sharing with others, entertaining strangers, considering others before oneself, honoring the accomplishments of others, etc. These all are outstanding examples of the scriptural "law of love" and are to be encour-aged. *Eph. 1:20-23, Col. 1:16-18, Phil. 2:9-11, 1Pet. 2:9-12, Gal. 2:20, 2Cor.5:17, Rom. 12:1-2, Rom. 1:5-6, Tit. 3:5, Gal. 2:16, Eph. 2:8-9, Rev.*

5:9, Heb. 9:22, Eph. 1:7-8, Eph. 2:12-13, 1Pet. 1:18-19, 2Thes. 2:15, Phil. 4:8-9.

Definitions:

By *biblical truth*, we mean the sole authority of the divine revelation of God to man, clearly inspirited by the Holy Spirit in the Holy Scriptures, and not what man thinks about God.

By *native religious traditionalism*, we mean the influence of the unwritten rules concerning spiritual conduct in our historical cultures which are not in accord with the revealed Word of God.

By *native culture*, we mean the dynamic learned lifeways, beliefs and values of our people as revealed in our languages, customs, relationships, arts and rituals. In native culture, religion permeates all aspects of life and is often identified as being the culture, even though it is only as aspect of it.

By *syncretism*, we refer specifically to the subtle attempt to integrate Biblical truth and faith in Christ with non-biblical Native religious beliefs, practices, and forms. The result is an adulteration of biblical truth and the birth of "another gospel (*Gal.1:6-9*)."

By *idolatry*, we mean exchanging the worship of the Creator for the worship of the creation. The Bible teaches that we must not "exchange the glory of the incorruptible God for an image in the form of corruptible man and of birds and four-footed animals and crawling creatures (*Ro.1:23*)."

APPENDIX:

B

(The following Appendix is a pamphlet given by CHIEF
Inc, used with permission by Rev. Huron Claus)

The Teaching of Biblical Truth and Traditional Indian Beliefs By Rev. Tom Claus[2]

Testimony

I am a Mohawk Indian, a member of the turtle clan
from the Six Nations reservation near Brantford
Ontario, Canada. I am a fourth generation Christian,
My great grandfather, Adam Elliot Thomas, a Six
Nation Council Chief was one of the first members

---

2 Rev. Tom Claus, *The Teaching of Biblical Truth and
Traditional Indian Beliefs*, (1644,Campo Bello Dr. Pheonix AZ
85022: CHIEF Inc. Copyright 1999) used with permission.

in our family to accept the Lord Jesus Christ as his personal Savior.

I gave my heart and life to Christ when I was fourteen years old. Soon after my conversion, I surrendered my life to preach the Gospel of Christ to my people. Now, for more than fifty years I've preached God's Word to my people in over 300 tribes from the Alaskan Natives to the South American Indians. I've seen many trust Christ as their Savior.

I always encourage my people to actively engage in four little talks every day to help them grow in their Christian life.

1. Talk to God (prayer)
2. Let God talk to you. (study the Bible)
3. Talk to someone about God. (witnessing)
4. Go where they talk about God. (attend church)

I trust this discipleship pamphlet will help give you more understanding and knowledge of Biblical truth as it compares to some of our traditional beliefs.

Tom Claus
President of CHIEF

Traditional Indian Beliefs	**Biblical Truth**
The Bible is a book written by men	The Bible is the inspired Word of God *Jn. 16:13-15, 2Tim. 3:16, 2Pet. 1:20, 21, Ro. 15:4*
God is the Great Spirit and has many spirit helpers.	God is One in three persons: Father, Son and Holy Spirit. *Mat.* 28:19; *Jn. 14:11; 15:26; 17:11*
Jesus Christ was a human being like any other man.	Jesus Christ is the eternal Son of God. *Mat. 3:17; 16:16; 27:54, Jn. 1:1-2*
The Indian's Church is the sacred places in nature.	The Christian's church is the body of believers in Christ Jesus. *1Cor. 12:13, Eph. 1:22;2:13-16; 4:4; 5:23; Col. 1:18, 24*

Traditional Indian Beliefs	**Biblical Truth**
Traditional Indian prayers use as mediators the creation, spirits, feathers and smoke.	The mediator for Christian prayers is the name of the Lord Jesus Christ. *Jn. 14:1-3,;26:23, Acts 4:12, Phil. 2:9-11*
Blood sacrifices are made of animals and birds to cleanse from all evil	Christ's blood alone can cleanse us from all sin. *Col. 1:13-14, Heb. 7:21; 9:12-14,28, 1Pet. 1:18-19*
The spirits came to our Indian people during fasting, dancing and ceremonies.	The Holy Spirit indwells, empowers, and equips all believers in Christ. *Jn. 14:16-18, Rom. 8:9-11,26, 1Cor. 12:13*
The evil spirits have power to bring sickness, curses and death.	The Holy Spirit is greater than all evil spirits and gives life. *Jn. 3:6-7; 17:15-19, 1Jn. 2:13; 4:4; 5:18*

Traditional Indian Beliefs	**Biblical Truth**
The traditional Indians` power is in medicine, fetishes and sacred objects	The Christian`s power is in the Holy Spirit and the authority of the scripture. *Ps. 119:89-90, Mat. 24:35, Rom. 3:2-4*
Good works will help you on your journey to the next world.	Christ`s finished work on the cross can save us and take us to heaven. *Jn. 3:16; 17:4, Gal. 1:4, Heb 9:26; 12:2*
Faith in the medicine man can free you from curses and evil.	Faith in Christ alone will set you free from sin and all its curse. *Jn. 8:36, Rom. 6:22; 8:2, Gal. 3:13; 5:1*
A covering of smoke of wood ashes will bring healing, cleansing and blessing.	The covering of Christ`s blood brings protection and blessing. *Rom. 3:24-25; 5:9, Eph. 1:7, Rev. 12:10-11*
The foundation of traditional Indian beliefs are legends and stories	The foundation of the Christian faith is the truth of God`s Word. *Ps. 119:160, Mat. 7:24-27, Luke 6:47-49 Jn. 14:6*

Traditional Indian Beliefs	Biblical Truth
The Indian world view is to live in harmony with nature.	The Christian`s world view is to live in harmony with God`s purupose for all men. *Acts 17:30, Rom. 8:28, Eph. 3:11-12, Heb 6:17-18, 2Pet. 3:9*
The way to God is through tobacco, peyote, sun, mountains, etc.	The way to God is through His Son, the Lord Jesus Christ. *Mat. 1:21, Jn. 14:6, Acts 4:12, 1Tim. 2:5, Heb. 9:15*
Traditional Indian culture is anthropcentric; man-centered.	Christian Indian culture is theocentric; (Christ) God-centered. *Eph. 2:8-9; 19:22, Phil. 3:7-9, 1Tim. 4:10*
Indian tradition teaches man is basically good.	The Bible teaches all men are sinners. *Isa. 53:6, Rom. 3:10-12,23; 5:12*

Traditional Indian Beliefs	Biblical Truth
Traditional beliefs are based on mystical and magical teaching.	The Christian faith is based on the clear sound doctrines of the Bible *Jn. 7:17-18; 16:13,14, 1Tim. 4:6, Titus 1:9*
Traditional beliefs teach man is equal with animals, birds and all of nature.	Man is superior to all of nature, because God made man a living soul and gave him a conscience, intellect, emotions and a will. *Gen.2:7, Mark 12:30, Jn. 1:12,13, Rom. 12:2, Heb 10:22*
Be generous give gifts, be kind and good to others and you will go to heaven.	Our gifts and good works will not save us. We must accept God`s gift of eternal life through Jesus Christ our Lord. *Rom. 3:10-12; 5:8; 6:23; 10:9-13, Titus 3:5*

End Notes

[1] *King James Version/Amplified Bible Parallel Edition (Grand Rapids, Michigan 49530, U.S.A. Zondervan copy right 1995) Romans 10:20*

[2] *King James Version, Holy Bible, Joel 2:28-29*

[3] *Norman Taylor. My Book My People: Our Kingdom (Copyright 1992 Taylor Publishing), pg 19*

[4] *Norman Taylor. n.p.*

[5] *Ibid*

[6] *Norman Taylor. pg 23*

[7] *Norman Taylor. pp 17-21*

[8] *Article written by Bishop Breynat and printed in the Toronto Star Weekly, May 28, 1938. Under the title, "La Tache La Plus Noire du Canadā", it appeared in a newspaper in Quebec City, Le Soleil, on July 3, 1938. Copies of it are retained by the Public Archives of Canada. RG85, vol. 310, also vol. 267, file 1003-2-1, and in the Minutes of the Northwest Territories Council, pp. 1363-1360.*

[9] *Norman Taylor. pg 33*

[10] *McCallum, Norman. Carrier of the Light Conference Prince George, B.C. June 2000 AD*

[11] *Norman Taylor. pg 34*

[12] *Norman Taylor. pg 35*

[13] *Norman Taylor. pp 58-61*

[14] *Norman Taylor. pg 37*

[15] *Josephus Complete Works Book Ten (Grand Rapids, Michigan, 49501, U.S.A. Lib. Congress # 60-15405 KREGAL PUBLICATIONS Published 1980, Copyright 1960, 1978), Chapter Nine – Ten, n.a.*

[16] *King James Version/Amplified Bible Parallel Edition (Grand Rapids, Michigan 49530, U.S.A. Zondervan copy right 1995)*

[17] *King James Version, Holy Bible, Daniel 1:3-7*

[18] *Holy Bible, Old Testament,*

[19] *Josephus Complete Works Book Ten. Chapter Nine – Ten*

[20] *Ibid n.p.*

[21] *King James Version, Holy Bible, Daniel 1:9, 19*

[22] *King James Version, Holy Bible, Esther*

[23] *Vines Complete Expository Dictionary of Old and New Testament Words. (Nashville, Tennessee by Thomas Nelson, Inc. Copyright 1984, 1996), pg 262*

[24] *Rosalie J. Slater. American Dictionary of the English Language (Renewal) (Chesapeake, Virginia P.O. Box 9588, 23321 Published by Foundation for American Christian Education copyright 1967, 1995). n.p.*

[25] *King James Version, Holy Bible, Daniel 5:6*

[26] *King James Version, Holy Bible, Nehemiah 2:1-9*

[27] *King James Version/Amplified Bible Parallel Edition*

[28] *Craig Smith, White Man's Gospel (Winnipeg, Manitoba: Indian Life Ministries, copy right 1994), pg 48*

[29] *King James Version/Amplified Bible Parallel Edition*

[30] *Edward Burnett Taylor. Primitive Culture (1871 – Britannica Article online Encyclopedia December 2005)*

[31] *Neil T Anderson. Living Free In Christ (Ventura, California: Regal Books, copyright 1993), pg 10*

[32] *John R Cross. The Stranger on the road to Emmaus 3rd ed. (Olds, AB: Good Seed International copyright 1997,1998, 1999, 2000, 2001, 2002, 2003, 2004), pg 69*

[33] *John R Cross. pg 75*

[34] *Neil T Anderson. pg 9*

[35] *Vines Complete Expository Dictionary of Old and New Testament Words. pg 262*

[36] *Rosalie J. Slater. n.p.*

[37] *Thomas King. Medicine River (90 Eglinton Avenue East, Suite 700, Toronto, Ontario, Canada M4P 2Y3: Penguin Group (Canada) copyright 1989), pp. 141-142*

[38] *Dr. Ronald Washington. Forgiveness and Reconciliation (Shippensburg, PA: Treasure House, copyright 1993), pp 11-13*

[39] *Garland Hunt. Racial Reconciliation (Charlotte, N.C.: Morning Star Publications) – video tape n.d.*

[40] *Rick Joyner. Overcoming Racism – Combating Spiritual Strongholds Series, (Charlotte, NC: Morning Star Publication copyright 1996), pp 7-8*

[41] *David Sitton To Every Tribe With Jesus – Understanding and Reaching Tribal Peoples for Christ (Sand Springs OK, Grace and Truth Books, 3406 Summit Boulevard 74063 Copyright 2005), pg. 91*

[42] *George Otis Jr. Twilight Labrynth (Grand Rapids, MI. Chosen Books copyright 1997), pg. 219*

[43] *David Sitton pg. 83*

[44] *Webster's II, New Riverside Dictionary, (One Beacon St. Boston MA. 02108 Houghton Mifflin Company Copyright 1984), pg. 183*

[45] *Ibid, pg. 127*

[46] *Scripture taken from the Holy Bible, New Life Version, copyright 1969, 1978,1983,1986,1992,199 7, Christian Literature International, P.O. Box 777, Canby, OR 97013. Used by permission."*

[47] *James Strong. Strong's Exhaustive Concordance of the Bible. (Peabody, MA P.O. Box 3473 01961-3473 Hendrickson Publishers) pg, 76*

[48] *The New Strong's Exhaustive Concordance of the Bible, (Nashville, Tennessee, by Thomas Nelson Inc., Publishers and distributed in Canada by Lawson Falle, Ltd., Cambridge, Ontario Thomas Nelson Publishers Copyright 1990), pp 105, 103*

[49] *James Strong. 43*

[50] *Ivan Doxtator. Identity Crises (Winnipeg, MO Conference: House Springs, Aug. 1998)*

[51] *Dr. Gary L. Greenwald. Seductions Exposed (Santa Ana, CA: Eagle's Nest Publications, Copyright 1988) n.p.*

[52] *Josephus Complete Works: Book 5 Chapter 3*

[53] *New Life Version*

[54] *New Life Version*

[55] *James Strong. pg. 43*

[56] *Nelson's Three-in-One Bible Reference Companion, (Nashville, Tennessee Thomas Nelson, Inc., Publishers copyright 1982), pg. 209*

[57] *James Strong. pg. 67*

[58] *James Strong. pg. 43*

[59] *The Strongest Strong's Exhaustive Concordance of the Bible, (Grand Rapids, Michigan, 49530 Zondervan Copyright 2001), pg. 1533*

[60] *James Strong. pg 68*

[61] *The Strongest Strong's Exhaustive Concordance of the Bible pg. 1533*

[62] *James Strong. pg. 7*

[63] *Nelson's Three-in-One Bible Reference Companion. pg. 726*

[64] *James Strong. pg. 54*

[65] *Nelson's Three-in-One Bible Reference Companion. pg.589*

[66] *James Strong. pg 54*

[67] *Nelson's Three-in-One Bible Reference Companion. pg. 502*

[68] *James Strong. pg 24*

[69] *The Strongest Strong's Exhaustive Concordance of the Bible pg.*

[70] *New Life Version*

[71] *Rick Warren, The Purpose-Driven Life (Grand Rapids, Michigan 49530 Zondervan Copyright 2002), pg. 66*

[72] *Nelson's Three-in-One Bible Reference Companion, pg. 748*

[73] *New Life Version*

[74] *Nelson's New Illustrated Bible Dictionary. (Nashville, Tennessee, By Thomas Nelson, Inc. Thomas Nelson Publishers Copyright 1995, 1986) pg. 895*

[75] *Ibid. pg. 500*

Printed in the United States
126554LV00001B/6/P

9 781604 777062